Amores Perros

Paul Julian Smith

 Publishing

A LOS QUE TAN AMABLE Y
GENEROSAMENTE ME
AYJDARON EN MÉXICO, D.F.:
EDGAR ESPEJEL, CARLOS
MONSIVÁIS, Y MARTHA SOSA

First published in 2003 by the
British Film Institute
21 Stephen Street, London W1T 1LN

Copyright © Paul Julian Smith 2003

The British Film Institute promotes greater
understanding and appreciation of,
and access to, film and moving image
culture in the UK.

British Library Cataloguing-in-Publication Data
A catalogue record for this book is available
from the British Library

ISBN 0-85170-973-7

Series design by Andrew Barron &
Collis Clements Associates

Typeset in Italian Garamond and Swiss 721BT
by D R Bungay Associates, Burghfield, Berks

Printed in Great Britain by
Cromwell Press, Trowbridge, Wiltshire

£8·99

BFI Modern Classics

Rob White
Series Editor

This book is to be returned on or before the last date stamped below or you will be charged a fine

ots

Contents

Prologue: Mexico City, 2002

The sun burns through the haze in this city of superlatives. The oldest, highest and most dynamic capital in Latin America is also the most populous metropolis on the planet, with some twenty million inhabitants. Two years after his election brought to an end seventy-one years of rule by the Institutional Revolutionary Party (PRI), President Vicente Fox of the rightist National Action Party (PAN) claims that Mexico cannot blame globalisation for its continuing economic crisis. He hints at the privatisation of electricity and water. The problems of poverty, illiteracy and corruption remain as urgent as ever. But if Fox still speaks of 'change' (a key word since before the election) one social issue has shifted against the wishes of his minority government: the Supreme Court has just ruled that abortion will now be legal in some limited circumstances.

National issues resurface in the most unlikely places. In the gossip magazines stars of the locally produced telenovelas that dominate TV schedules – and are Mexico's most distinctive form of popular narrative – debate for and against abortion. And while the soaps are advertised with tag lines of familiar extravagance ('Passion, betrayal, fury, love!'), new social issues are breaking through into a traditional form. Dominant network Televisa launches an unashamedly romantic melodrama (*Entre el amor y el odio/Between Love and Hate*), in a time slot where rival channel Azteca has scheduled the relatively realistic *Agua y aceite/Oil and Water*, which explores such unaccustomed topics as drug trafficking, artificial insemination and lesbianism. And if the press and television tirelessly discuss the loves, hates and marriages of wealthy local celebrities, real life provides melodramas more bizarre than the soaps: pop idol Gloria Trevi, who fled Mexico after being accused with her manager of paedophilia, has fallen pregnant in a Brazilian jail and may therefore escape extradition.

New national narratives thus suggest new forms of gender and sexual relations. Meanwhile the problems of the city remain the same. Whole areas are 'abandoned', with the highest rates of drug consumption and car theft being in those with the fewest facilities for recreation. In the Doctores *colonia* or neighbourhood, where twenty-two street gangs have been identified, it is proposed to build football pitches to distract unemployed youth from crime. Elsewhere a salesman is stripped, strangled and his body burned on a street corner. The city debates opening a new rubbish tip (the current one will soon be full) and adding a second tier to its expressways in order to alleviate notorious traffic jams. In the sedate southern suburb of Coyoacán, the pretty square has been refurbished and benefits from private security. On inner city streets, however, Mexicans are advised not to buy food from ubiquitous vendors, lest they be exposed to typhoid.

City of social contrasts, Mexico also gives rise to clashes of sound and vision. At 6 a.m. and 6 p.m. the army drums and bugles mark the unfurling of a huge flag in the central square of the Zócalo. But the historic centre is also the venue for Aztec drumming and dancing, with participants donning colourful feathered headdresses. Newspaper kiosks display graphic contrasts, juxtaposing posters of Christ and Spiderman, or the dark-skinned Virgin of Guadalupe and the blonde, pouting Britney Spears. Sharp-suited businessmen from yuppie areas like Condesa rub shoulders with gaily dressed indigenous saleswomen and pristine schoolgirls, sporting characteristic ankle socks.

If the keywords of the moment are 'change' and 'democratisation' then the arts are not unaffected. After decades of paternalist corruption, it is decided that local artists will contribute directly to a new Secretariat of Culture in the capital. The current head says that to separate culture from politics what is needed is not civil servants, dependent on one political party, but rather the direct participation of citizens. Cinema is also urgently in need of reform. While commentators lament the decline of production to some twenty-five features a year (and some associate this decadence with the malign influence of government funding bodies), four varied Mexican features are being screened at the capital's theatres. *Inspiración/Inspiration* is a teen romantic comedy (featuring soap star Arath de la Torre), set around the restaurants and swimming pools of the southern suburbs. The only trace of social problems is a brief appearance by an Indian child selling roses at the kerb side. *Un mundo raro/A Weird World* (directed by Armando Casas *et al.*) is a satire on television, funded by an alphabet soup of public bodies including IMCINE (the national film institute) and UNAM (the national university). Here a young gangster wheedles his way on to a comedy show after kidnapping the immoral host. More challenging is *Vivir mata/Living Kills* (by veteran Nicolás Echevarría). A would-be novelist recounts, while stuck in an epic traffic jam, how he spent a night of love with an eccentric radio announcer. This relatively high-budget film features frequent helicopter shots of city skyscrapers, even as it appeals to an apocalyptic rhetoric of the Aztec end of days. The reviewer in respected journal *Letras Libres* wrote that the caricatures and overacting in this urban comedy made him weep. Finally *Corazones rotos/Broken Hearts* (Rafael Montero) is an ensemble drama focusing on the middle-class inhabitants of a single apartment building: the bourgeois matron who learns of her husband's insolvency only when he has a heart attack; the religious fanatics who prefer a suicide pact to eviction; the alienated son of an incestuous prostitute who courts suicide by balancing precariously on the roof of the building.

What all of these films share, despite their wildly varying tones and ambitions, is the city itself. And as a place of encounter and conflict, Mexico City's cinemas are as diverse as its social classes. The newly built Cinemex Real Cinema on the central avenue of the Paseo de la Reforma is a glamorous multiplex with state of the art sound and vision: gliding up the escalators filmgoers have an excellent view of the city through plate-glass windows. At the other end of the Alameda Park, just fifteen minutes walk away, is the Mariscala, a huge decrepit shell, which shows two films for the price of one cheap ticket. Unlike the relatively discreet well-heeled habitués of the Real, the Mariscala's humble customers take over the theatre for their own purposes: poor mothers chat as their children play in the filthy aisles. A place of extreme contrasts, Mexico City is also a prize location for a cinema of extremes.

1 Everything Changes ...

3.– EXTERIOR STREET DAY

[Octavio] puts his foot down on the accelerator once more. The Topaz pulls alongside them. There are three men inside it. The man in the back takes out a gun and aims. Octavio swerves violently, passes a bus on the inside and leaves them behind. The traffic lights turn red. When it looks like the Caribe will get through, a golden Honda Accord comes out from a side street and smashes into them on the right-hand side. The Caribe spins around and starts to turn over. The Accord is shattered, continues straight ahead and smashes against the pavement. The Caribe is left with its tyres face up on the traffic island. FADE OUT[1]

One regular performer in the Zócalo square of Mexico City ('D.F.' to locals) is an old man, with long grey hair and unkempt beard, who marshals a troupe of performing dogs for the informal audience that gathers around him. Dogs are everywhere in D.F., or so it would seem. In the splendid museum of the Templo Mayor (the main Aztec temple) is a grotesque sculpture of Xolótl, dog-headed god of the double, the deformed and the monstrous. The black-eyed canine, known in Nahuatl as 'itzcuintli', also serves as one of the symbols in the Aztec calendar. Smooth-skinned domesticated dogs look out from Diego Rivera's famous murals of the conquest in the Palacio Nacional. The most bizarre of the current crop of telenovelas (*Cómplices al rescate del amor/Accomplices to the Rescue of Love*) features not only the predictable premise of identical twins separated at birth, but also the unlikely device of a talking dog, who takes a bullet for its master. Televisa programmed a series of films with a canine theme under the banner 'Amor es perros' ('Love is dogs'). 'Amores perros' is also used by a gossip magazine as a caption for a photo of a blonde star at a private party, caressing her retriever, as golden as its glamorous mistress.

Two years after its release in June 2000 *Amores Perros*, a title translating as both 'lousy love affairs' and, more literally, 'dog loves', has thus become proverbial in Mexico. The winner of over thirty awards (including the most successful film at the Mexican box office of its year), *Amores Perros* is widely credited with kick-starting a Mexican film industry which was in ruins and heralding a renaissance for the national audiovisual sector. Abroad, *Amores Perros* was sold to territories around the world and played for some six months in London, a city where Latin American cinema is scarcely seen. Yet this exceptional success was hardly to be expected and indeed took its creators by surprise. It was the first feature for young director Alejandro González Iñárritu, for the rising star of its ensemble cast, twenty-year-old Gael García Bernal, and for its executive producer Martha Sosa. As an autodidact who did not attend the national film school, González Iñárritu was outside the system of patronage traditional in the Mexican cultural field, as throughout society; and as new private companies his Zeta Films and Sosa's Altavista received no government support. Moreover the brutal subject matter of dogfighting and the extended length of 153 minutes made commercial

The promotional sticker

success seem implausible. A closer study of the history of *Amores Perros*'s production, promotion and reception reveals the secrets of its success, which relate to the vexed question of *mexicanidad*, or what it means to be Mexican.

A 'case study' of the production process, confirmed as accurate by producer Martha Sosa, appeared in trade journal *Screen International*.[2] The pitch was simple: 'the impact of a car crash on three disparate groups of people'. The first stage (mid-1997 to spring 1998) was the meeting between screenwriter and novelist Guillermo Arriaga and González Iñárritu (known to friends and colleagues familiarly as 'El Negro'). Although González Iñárritu had made no feature he had considerable experience and success as a radio DJ and producer and as a director of TV commercials. He also had one TV pilot to his name. Arriaga and González Iñárritu teamed up with the intention of 'exploring the theme of human frailty', using dogs as a central motif. They were approached by Sosa, development executive of new Mexican mini-studio Altavista (also with a background in pop music promotion), who secured 'first read' on the eventual script. The second stage (July 1998) was the intense collaboration between writer, director and producers. A 170-page first draft of the script was trimmed and polished by Arriaga, González Iñárritu, Sosa and Francisco González Compeán, director general of Altavista, who would also be an executive producer. All agreed on the main issues:

The film will be structured around three loosely-connected stories linked by a car accident; it will use documentary-style camerawork, with the film stock processed with silver retention to create stronger contrasts and texture in colour; the dog fights will not be explicit and the dogs will be handled with extreme care; the cast will largely consist of unknowns; and there will be a strong soundtrack.[3]

In November 1998 the film was greenlit by Altavista's powerful parent companies CIE and Sinca Inbrusa. Already it was seen as a 'launch pad for Mexican talent' into the world, setting a standard both in production values and film-making. The 'visceral' subject matter was worrying; but the film acquired in-house funding for its $2.4 million budget: 86 per cent from Altavista and 14 per cent from González Iñárritu's own production company Zeta Films.

The ten-week shoot took place entirely on location in Mexico City from April to June 1999. The process was risky: at the opening car crash (a complex shot requiring nine cameras) one vehicle smashed into a parked taxi by mistake. In the dogfight scenes the dogs wore transparent braces inside their mouths so they could not bite each other. Anticipating controversy, the producers included footage on how these scenes were shot in the electronic press kit (EPK). Distribution in Mexico would be

Alejandro González Iñárritu

with NuVisión, a sister company of Altavista; international distribution was acquired by Lion's Gate, just after the film was selected for Critics' Week at Cannes (June 1999–April 2000). Taking the top prize in its competition at Cannes, *Amores Perros* provoked a 'buying frenzy' and was sold to France, Italy, Spain and Israel. Opening in Mexico in June it would be the second highest-grossing domestic film ever, taking $10 million. González Iñárritu also won best new director at the Edinburgh festival, thus helping to ensure distribution in the UK, a notoriously tricky territory for non-English-language cinema (May–August 2000).

Finally *Amores Perros* was nominated in the best foreign film category for both the Golden Globes and Academy Awards, thus securing a 'strong buzz' in the US. Released at the end of March 2001, by early July it had grossed $5 million in the US and $20 million worldwide. Nevertheless the film hit censorship problems in Germany and the UK because of its subject matter. Although the RSPCA filed a complaint to the British Board of Film Classification, *Amores Perros* was passed without cuts after the distributor Optimum Releasing, using the footage from the EPK, convinced the board that the dogs were not harmed. Opening in the UK in May 2001, it took $680,000 in five weeks.

Making the film a 'launch pad for Mexican talent' abroad was part of the production process from a very early stage. Press files and private documentation from Altavista reveal how the promotional strategy and audience response in Mexico itself also fed on national ambition and recognition. In private conversation Martha Sosa told me (13 February 2002) that there were two vital moments in *Amores Perros*'s reception: Cannes and the Oscars. In both, Altavista used its promotional expertise to expert effect. *Amores Perros* entered Cannes in competition for the Critics' Week rather than the main prize in the belief that 'the best competition is the one you win' (not necessarily the most prestigious). In its campaign to be selected for the Oscars, the company engaged a Los Angeles publicist who specialised in the foreign film category and was rewarded as one of the five nominees out of entries from over forty countries. Although González Iñárritu claimed in the press that 'tigers are strong but dogs are smarter', he did not expect to beat *Crouching Tiger,*

Hidden Dragon for the award itself. The Mexican team were content with nomination, which they claimed was the first for their country for over twenty years.

Mexican press coverage focused on the ambiguous relationship between national production and international reception. Let us begin with Cannes (Sosa's first vital moment), when the film was still unknown at home. On the one hand, journalists stressed the 'tremendous *mexicanidad*' of the film (*Cine Mundial*, 2 May 2000) and González Iñárritu defended Mexican cinema (*El Heraldo*, 14 May 2000). *Esto* (20 May 2000) reported that 'González Iñárritu [spoke] in Cannes about Mexicans': 'We want to see ourselves reflected ... to show the complex mosaic of an enormous city such as Mexico and make it live like an anthropological experiment.' On the other hand, this 'experiment' is modified by Mexicans' knowledge of foreigners' ignorance of their culture and locals' awareness of the obstacles that culture faces abroad. So González Iñárritu also claimed in Cannes that 'for the Europeans Mexican cinema is a strange world' (*La Crónica*, 20 May 2000), and that it was 'ridiculous' that a country of one hundred million inhabitants could make only twenty-five features a year (*Sol de Mediodía*, 20 May 2000). More controversially he noted that *Amores Perros* 'reflects the degree of rottenness to be found in our society' (*Novedades*, 20 May 2000). There is a curious contradiction here. National pride and shame go hand in hand. Indeed pride comes in part from exhibition of that shame to an international audience, from the attempt to demonstrate that the new Mexico is adult enough to face up to its political and social problems. External consecration precedes and promotes internal institutionalisation: later *Amores Perros* would be the first film to be shown in the season of free autumn screenings on a giant screen in the Zócalo square, the symbolic heart of the nation (*Esto*, 5 October 2000).

Sosa's second key moment is the Oscar competition (which took place after the Mexican premiere). The press crowed that, with *Before Night Falls* and *Traffic* also in competition, 'this year's ceremony has a marked Hispanic accent' (*El Universal*, 25 March 2001); and, punning on the title, claimed that 'Amor es ... un Oscar' ('Love is ... an Oscar') (*El*

Imparcial, 25 March 2001). Yet there was also a nervous and defiant awareness of the particularity, even incongruity, of the film in a US context. *Sol de México* reacted indignantly to the frequent comparison of *Amores Perros* with Quentin Tarantino's *Pulp Fiction* (13 April 2001); *Reforma* responded more humorously with a graphic of Cofi (the vicious mongrel of the first and third episodes) sitting in his red seat at the ceremony between place cards reading 'Tom Hanks' and 'Julia Roberts' (25 March 2001). *Amores Perros* may be star Gael García's 'passport to the whole world' (*El Norte*, 29 April 2001) and may have made González Iñárritu 'unstoppable and international' (*Reforma*, 1 May 2001), but still Mexico is the ghost at the feast, the big black dog at the glamorous soirée of global cinema.

    Reforma featured another graphic of Cofi, this time with an Ariel statuette in his mouth, when it came to the forty-third annual Mexican film awards (29 May 2001). Nominated in fifteen categories, *Amores Perros* took a record eleven prizes. Once more national and international acclaim proved inseparable. At the ceremony held at the Aztec art deco Palacio de Bellas Artes by the Alameda Park in the heart of Mexico City, González Iñárritu claimed modestly that he had not expected to win, since he was a 'prophet in his own country' (*México Hoy*, 30 May 2001). Confirming that he did not intend to head for Hollywood, he also noted that what was needed in Mexico was a continuity that would allow directors to keep working in their own country. In a demonstration of local star quality, Gael García (also 'wanted by Hollywood', according to the Mexican press) arrived surrounded by bodyguards and greeted by hordes of screaming fans (*Reforma*, 29 and 30 May 2001). Striking a less optimistic note was Jorge Fons, director of government film agency IMCINE. He recited the alarming fluctuations in recent feature production, reported by the press as eleven in 1998, nineteen in 1999, fifty in 2000, and just four in the first five months of 2001 (*Esto*, 30 May 2001). Stressing national pride once more, he affirmed that 'cinema in Mexico must be [a question of] culture and of dignity' (*El Financiero*, 29 May 2001).

    Amores Perros, a private production, had triumphed against all the odds and outside the public context of film support and development

represented by Fons. Indeed it is Martha Sosa's belief that the success of
the film came precisely from its novelty. Premiered just two weeks before
the elections which spelled the end of over seventy years of rule by the
established PRI, the film benefited from a public mood that made
'change' ('cambio') the key word of the moment. Indeed, for Sosa the
moral of the film is that, after a chance car crash, 'everything changes' for
all the characters. Of course the lengthy production process could not
have anticipated the happy accident of *Amores Perros*'s release at a time of
unprecedented national transition. Sosa puts it down to 'collective
unconscious'. However, the Mexican release was brought forward to
16 June 2000 in order to benefit from the success at Cannes, which was
received by the local press as if Mexico had won the World Cup. While the
distributor had expected to launch the film with forty prints, it was
eventually released with an exceptional 220.

But if the timing was intuitive, the domestic marketing left nothing
to chance.[4] Altavista had already paid for five Mexican journalists to
attend Cannes, in the hope of awards, and had through its sister radio
stations organised a contest whose prize was a trip to the festival for a local
film fan. The premiere at the huge Teatro Metropólitan on 13 June spared
no expense. Three thousand four hundred guests partied at a fiesta,
entertained by bands that had featured on the soundtrack. Teaser trailers
were played four times a day at Hard Rock Cafes throughout the nation
and a spot on MTV promoted a link from Levi's web page to
amoresperros.com. Promotion proclaimed that *Amores Perros* was a
'Winner at Cannes 2000' (without specifying the Critics' Week
competition in which it had won its awards). Postcards featuring the tag
line ('Love is …') and stark stickers in black, white and red appeared
everywhere. Materials distributed included: 5,000 T-shirts, 1,000 baseball
caps, 500 watches, 1,500 posters and 2,000 handsome press kits.
Meanwhile González Iñárritu, a media professional skilled in TV, radio
and advertising, gave interviews on his return from Cannes to twenty
Mexican magazines, five colour supplements, two major newspapers,
twenty-six radio programmes and ten TV shows. As specialist magazine
Cine XS wrote, if *Amores Perros* is representative of a 'new trend' in

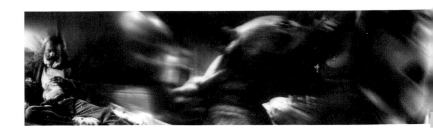

Images from the promotional pressbook

Octavio puts his foot down

The Latin American Tower

The man takes out a gun

The cars crash

The trail of a dead dog

Octavio's finger

Blood on the hot plate

Valeria on the poster

Susana, Ramiro and the Walkman

Octavio's crowded room

Octavio and Mauricio on the roof

Mauricio's statue of Venus

Octavio, Susana and the mirror

The greenish hue of night scenes

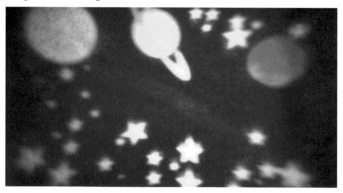

Daniel's daughters' night light

The bloody blade on the pavement

Maru's splashes of colour

Daniel and Valeria

El Chivo and Maru

Daniel and Valeria's dream apartment

El Chivo spies on Luis in the restaurant

Mexican cinema it is not just because its 'quality' makes it able to compete throughout the world; it is because the 'professionalisation' of its marketing requires generous investment in press campaigns, promotion and festivals.[5]

Not everyone was seduced by the media blitz, however. Jorge Ayala Blanco, a prolific film scholar and caustic film critic for the business daily *El Financiero*, wrote that the blame for the film's supposed artistic failures lies in its 'choque' (both 'car crash' and 'shock' in Spanish). Sarcastically reiterating the 'shocking' elements of the film, Ayala claimed *Amores Perros* was a 'success prefabricated by the technomarketing, Fox-style strategy, a tridramatic soap opera'.[6] The parallelisms among the three narratives lacked clarity, the use of silver on the negative was 'abusive', the hand-held camera 'nauseating', and the moral banal: humans are animal, love is ... dogs ('Amor es ... perros'). Finally, he found the characters stereotypical ('lumpen proletariat or dominant class with nothing in the middle') and the vision of D.F. 'grotesque' ('spaces without places and places without spaces').[7] Curiously enough all of these criticisms were contradicted by another well-known critic, Leonardo García Tsao. Reporting from Cannes for the leftist *La Jornada*, García Tsao stressed the film's 'desire to tell a story beyond all other elements'; claimed the film was by no means 'artificial' in spite of González Iñárritu's background in advertising; and praised the 'solid screenplay, convincing cast, and [ability] to sustain dramatic tension' through a lengthy running time.[8]

Ayala's petulance was probably a response to *Amores Perros*'s unprecedented publicity campaign. But it also marked an attempt by an established critic to distance himself from the taste of the crowd and thus conserve his own distinctive authority. Ayala is not above exploiting *Amores Perros* for his own promotional purposes, however: his latest collection of reviews bears a still from the film he so detests on its cover. Beyond production and promotion, then, these contradictory critical responses suggest that *Amores Perros* only makes sense when seen in the broader context of Mexican cultural consumption.

Néstor García Canclini has traced the changes that have recently produced 'new spectators' in Mexico. Cinema audiences declined rapidly,[9] but film viewing rose, with increasing access to features on TV and video (invariably rented). Theatres remained important as a mode of exhibition, however, with mature provincial audiences still regarding cinemagoing as part of a social 'ritual', involving a stroll and visit to a restaurant or café;[10] while urban youth, albeit less formal, are faithful also. Interestingly enough there is a positive correlation between educational level and a preference for viewing local films in theatres.[11] The dominance of US video, however, is evident in Mexican branches of Blockbusters, which display Hollywood films by genre (with their national origin unspecified), reserving only a tiny space for nationally defined 'foreign films', including Latin American.[12] It is perhaps no accident that Blockbusters is a crucial location for *Amores Perros*: yuppie businessman Luis is kidnapped by hit man El Chivo when leaving the garish glass and neon store.

García Canclini notes that there is a 'polarisation of publics' with critics tending to support minority or elitist tastes that are not shared by the mass audience. But in spite of these structural drawbacks, some Mexican titles remain successful. He concludes with a prediction that foreshadows the unprecedented success of *Amores Perros*:

The wide demand for [Mexican] films which treat historical themes and contemporary social problems proves that light entertainment is not the exclusive reason for watching cinema. For many sectors [of the public], especially amongst younger demographics and those benefiting from higher education, the problematic treatment of current issues, close to everyday life, not to mention intercultural questions and artistic innovations, may increase attendance [at cinemas].[13]

From the first moments of its breathtaking opening sequence (the dazzling car chase), *Amores Perros* clearly makes a bid for this new, sophisticated audience. Addressing the most urgent social themes of the day (poverty, corruption and violence) and artistically innovative in its complex plotting and stylised cinematography, González Iñárritu's feature appeared 'naturally' to fill the gap in the market identified by García Canclini for intelligent, youth-oriented domestic fare. Beyond any 'collective unconscious', the film's success at home testifies to a magical matching between the subjective dispositions of the artist (the aesthetic preferences of the production team) and the objective positions of the audience (the needs of a national public at a specific historical moment). *Amores Perros* proved a perfect fit for Mexico's peculiar circumstances at the time.

Recent research confirms this. Patricia Torres San Martín has carried out detailed and valuable analysis of *Amores Perros*'s audience on its release in Guadalajara.[14] She discovered that most of the viewers were aged between eighteen and twenty-five, educated and of the middle class. Like the Mexican press reporting from Cannes and Hollywood, audiences volunteered a new national pride as a reason for seeing the film ('We've had enough gringo shit and now Mexican cinema is giving us great stuff'). They also enjoyed the unusual plot structure ('three stories in one') and the film's mimetic success ('it reflects the society we live in'). The true split in the audience is along class lines. Working-class viewers said the film was 'sadistic', 'sad', even 'disgusting': 'they always put Mexico down'. Middle-class spectators could afford to keep a distance from the subject matter: 'I liked it because it shows the raw reality of Mexico City, especially of the bad neighbourhoods'; 'It reflects the culture of poverty.' Interestingly, audiences seemed to forget the very existence of the second narrative of the film, the bourgeois drama of model Valeria. Two young women of middle-class origin were dismissive, saying this character represented 'the banality and perversity of the construction of female beauty'. Another witness in the same demographic confesses she was 'ashamed' to think that such an 'ugly' image of Mexico could be shown to Europe. The history of *Amores Perros*'s production, promotion and reception reveals that it is truly a national phenomenon, however ambivalent. What remains to be seen is how that phenomenon intersects with narrative forms, both local and global.

2 The Dictatorship of Tears

Mexico City, the present. Teenage Octavio speeds through the city streets with his friend Jorge, pursued by gun-toting gangsters and with a bloody Rottweiler in the back seat. There is a spectacular car crash. In flashback we discover the causes of the crash. Octavio lives in poverty with his long-suffering mother, brutal brother Ramiro, timid sister-in-law Susana and her sickly baby. Octavio falls in love with Susana and the couple start to have sex. In order to get the money to go off together, Octavio enters his dog Cofi in illegal fights run by fat Mauricio. Ramiro, meanwhile, is carrying out armed robberies. Jealous Octavio has his brother brutally beaten. Returning home one day, Octavio finds Ramiro and Susana have left, taking most of the money with them. Octavio stakes his remaining winnings on a last fight against the dog of vicious gangster El Jarocho. When the latter shoots Cofi, Octavio knifes him in the stomach. With this we return to the opening car chase and crash.

Before the crash Octavio and Jorge had glimpsed the glamorous Spanish model Valeria on TV with her poodle, Richi. We now flashback

to the studio. Valeria's wealthy married lover Daniel has just bought her a handsome apartment. Setting off in her car to buy champagne, Valeria is seriously wounded in the car crash, her leg shattered. When she returns to the new flat, depressed and in great pain, she is in a wheelchair. Richi goes down a hole and is trapped beneath the parquet floor. Daniel and Valeria now argue bitterly as they try over several days to release him. One night Daniel returns to discover Valeria unconscious on the floor. This time her leg has to be

Valeria's perverse beauty

amputated. Daniel, distraught, rips up the floor and retrieves the wounded poodle.

We now cut to another speeding car. Bent cop Leonardo is driving with yuppie businessman, Gustavo. The latter has a rendezvous with the dishevelled El Chivo, an ex-terrorist who now lives in squalor with his dogs and works as a hitman. El Chivo agrees to kill Gustavo's half-brother and business partner, Luis. As he stalks Luis, El Chivo witnesses the car crash. He takes the wounded Cofi home. Meanwhile cop Leonardo foils a bank robbery led by Ramiro, who is shot dead. Octavio confronts Susana at his brother's funeral, but she refuses to go off with him. El Chivo is devastated to find that Cofi has killed his other dogs. Rather than shooting Luis, he brings him back to his home, where he also lures Gustavo. Taunting the two half-brothers, he ties them up, gives them a gun and, after washing and shaving, abandons them and his home for good. Leaving a message on his daughter's answerphone in which he tells her his true life story (she believes him to be dead), El Chivo sets off on foot into a wasteland on the outer limits of the city, accompanied only by the dog Cofi.

The most unusual feature of *Amores Perros*'s narrative structure is its division into three parts. Each part is signalled by intertitles referring to the diverse relationships it treats: an impoverished young man and his sister-in-law ('Octavio and Susana'); an adulterous magazine editor and his supermodel girlfriend ('Daniel and Valeria'); and, finally, a leftist guerrilla turned contract killer and the daughter he abandoned long ago ('El Chivo and Maru'). Patricia Torres notes that audiences in Guadalajara, whatever their level of education or social background, appeared to have little difficulty in following this complex narrative pattern, even though there are few Mexican precedents for it (she cites only Arturo Ripstein's *La mujer del puerto*/*The Woman of the Port* [1997] and *El callejón de los milagros*/*Miracle Alley* [1994] by future head of IMCINE, Jorge Fons). One reason for the familiarity of such a structure, rejected angrily by many Mexican supporters of the film (including executive producer Martha Sosa), is that it is reminiscent of *Pulp Fiction*.

Quentin Tarantino's celebrated ensemble piece also consists of three main narrative strands brought together not by a car crash, but by a hold-up in a diner. The opening sequence of *Reservoir Dogs*, in which gangsters attempt to staunch the bleeding of a comrade in the back seat of a car, is also apparently similar to the first scene of *Amores Perros*, in which it is Cofi who lies wounded in the speeding car.

González Iñárritu himself has preferred to cite forerunners such as John Cassavetes, Lars Von Trier and Wong Kar wai. And Sosa is surely right when she says that comparisons with Tarantino reveal an ignorance of Mexican cultural context, not to mention a deafness to tone. Moreover it is not hard to find local precedents for *Amores Perros* in the Mexican 'New Cinema' of the 1970s and the telenovela which has dominated Latin American TV screens for some fifty years. Both genres are obsessed with *mexicanidad*, but their definitions of its scope do not always overlap. Just as García Canclini and Torres provide some explanation for the national success of *Amores Perros* among changing audiences, so studies of New Cinema and telenovela allow us to read narrative structure sympathetically for national resonance, without rushing to compare the film with overfamiliar, but inappropriate, models from Hollywood.

One paradox of *Amores Perros* is that it combines a directly visceral effect with an oblique and intellectual construction. A specific

The dogfight

explanation for this curious mixture is the personalities of the two main creative collaborators: romantic director González Iñárritu and cerebral screenwriter Guillermo Arriaga. More generally it is often hard to separate emotion from narrative form. Symmetries and repetitions configure the shapes of many films, working on different levels. This is particularly the case with a plot as complex as that of *Amores Perros*. At the surface level the three episodes are, of course, united by dogs: Octavio's black mongrel Cofi, Valeria's white poodle Richi and El Chivo's family of pets, slaughtered when he takes in Cofi after the latter is wounded in the car crash. But from the beginning of the production process the dogs were seen as a mere motif disguising the true theme of 'human frailty'. At this thematic level, beyond the detail of each episode, further patterns emerge. All three episodes explore infidelity: Octavio commits adultery with his brother's wife, as does Daniel with a woman younger and more beautiful than his spouse. Luis, the businessman El Chivo is contracted to kill, is bedding a married colleague and apparently screwing over his half-brother, Gustavo, at their common workplace. The latter, in turn, betrays Luis by attempting to procure his death. Arguably, at a further level of abstraction, the episodes are united by poetic justice: the ambitions of Octavio, Daniel and Gustavo, which elicit variable degrees of sympathy in the audience, are all thwarted. Faithlessness does not pay.

An example will make this clear. Towards the end of the film El Chivo returns to his squalid home: trash is piled in the corners of the entrance, pale light slinks diagonally through the shutters. The convalescent Cofi, recently adopted by El Chivo after he found him at the car crash, comes into shot on the right and shuffles up to him. There is a cut to an extreme close-up of the mongrel's matted black coat. El Chivo caresses the dog, but pulls up his hand to find his fingers are covered in blood. Walking quickly inside he turns on the light. A slow pan from his point of view reveals his dead pets strewn on the floor. El Chivo kneels down, desperately willing them to live and invoking their pathetic names: Flor ('Flower') and Frijol ('Bean'). Swiftly drawing his pistol, El Chivo takes aim at the incomprehending mongrel, who stares blankly into the camera.

This dramatic moment is a direct visual echo of a much earlier scene in the film when Cofi is threatened with a gun by Octavio's brother Ramiro. The surface similarity links the two episodes. But, typically, this is repetition with a twist. At a deeper level, the scenes are quite different. Ramiro never learns the true consequences of violence and will end up dead in a shoot-out. For El Chivo, on the other hand, this will prove a turning point. Sparing Cofi, he will give up contract killing and attempt to begin a new life.

The last version of Guillermo Arriaga's script, which remains unpublished in the Spanish and is dated to just before the shoot began (30 March 1999), still bears the working title 'Black Dog/White Dog' ('Perro negro/perro blanco'). The threefold narrative structure is here undercut by a value system based on doubles: black and white, rich and poor, good and bad. And a closer look at the format of the script reveals that the narrative structure is not as symmetrical as might first appear. As José Arroyo noted in his review in *Sight and Sound*,[15] the time scheme is skewed and 'the periods before and after the crash [are] given different weight in each section'. Moreover, in the script the three episodes are not originally allotted the same number of scenes: Octavio and Susana are given 1–75; Valeria and Daniel 76–132; and El Chivo and Maru 133–82. In the film itself this imbalance is more pronounced because a large number of

Ramiro, Susana's husband

sequences in the second story did not survive the final cut. (Some of these scenes are included as an extra on the DVD.)

A further imbalance in the original script is in the interpenetration of the three strands. While Octavio and Susana are interrupted only three times by Daniel and Valeria, there are seven cutaways to El Chivo, mostly towards the start of the script. Once again this imbalance is exaggerated in the film itself, where sequence 9 (which introduces Daniel in the car with his wife and daughters) is postponed until sequence 29. As we watch the first half-hour of *Amores Perros*, then, El Chivo is quickly established as a brooding and enigmatic presence, while Daniel remains relatively invisible.

Crucial to narrative coherence are those scenes in which characters from more than one episode coincide. Valeria, glimpsed on a poster earlier, first appears live on a TV show watched by Octavio just before the final dog fight (script sequence 70). The audience is subtly prepared for the second episode (subtly, because none of the other programmes glimpsed on Octavio's television will acquire narrative relevance). The first and the third narratives are obliquely combined in scene 115: Octavio's brother Ramiro holds up a bank where Leonardo, the bent cop who procures customers for El Chivo, is cashing a cheque. Similarly, the final combination (second and third episodes) occurs briefly at the end of an episode: El Chivo drives his beaten-up van past Valeria's poster, which is being taken down (no. 176). This is one of those symmetrical patterns which are imperceptible to an audience already disoriented by the flashback framing device.

This kind of repetition creates resonance and pathos. For example, as we read the script or watch the film we experience the four versions of one act (the car crash) in completely different ways. In the first (no. 3) we have only just met Octavio and his friend Jorge, with whom we have travelled in the vertiginous car chase. By the second (no. 75) we are familiar with the motive for the chase (Octavio's stabbing of hoodlum El Jarocho after he had shot fighting dog Cofi). The third version is seen from Valeria's perspective. On this red-letter day (she has just discovered her boyfriend has finally left his wife), she sets out for celebratory wine, absent-mindedly singing along to a catchy pop song, pausing to reapply lipstick before the lights change (no. 81). A fade to black mercifully shields us (and her) from the carnage. The final version (no. 142) is seen from El Chivo's perspective and this time it is merciless: we are shown the bloody remains of Octavio's dead friend Jorge, Octavio's own wounded body carried into the street, and Valeria's anguish trapped behind the wheel. The power of this scene relies not only on the resonance acquired through repetition or the shock effect of graphic damage to human tissue. It comes also from the fact that this is the only scene of the 182 in the script in which characters from all three episodes coincide.

Clearly also the emotional potency of the final crash sequence derives, by this late point in the film, from our knowledge of the motivation of all the participants. It is here that sequences omitted from the script are valuable evidence for the minute attention to detail in the creative process of *Amores Perros*. The final cut consistently omits scenes with minor characters in all three episodes: Susana visits her drunken mother twice in the script (only once in the film); Daniel takes his two daughters to the park after he has left their mother (on the page, but not the screen); El Chivo pays a visit to his dead wife's sister (whom we see in the film only at the funeral scene). The loss of such supporting players and additional plot points tends, inevitably, to increase attention on the leads, isolating them from social and familial context.

This is most clearly the case in the second episode, the one with which González Iñárritu reportedly had most trouble. The claustrophobia of the single set (Valeria's new dream home) is heightened by the omission of the housekeeper engaged in the script by Daniel. It is interesting to note that as we watch the film itself we are not aware of this absence, in spite of the fact that Valeria is clearly unable to look after herself and that Daniel, irrespective of his financial difficulties, could surely afford the modest Mexican wage of domestic help. Valeria's isolation is further enhanced by her lack of back story. Film spectators take the love affair for granted and do not enquire into the characters' past; readers of the script learn, to their surprise, that Valeria has aborted a child fathered by Daniel. The disappearance of her pampered pooch (to whom she refers on the TV show as her 'child') thus takes on a deeper resonance: this is not the first baby she has lost. In spite of the brilliant versatility of Goya Toledo's

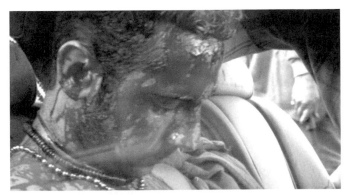

Octavio's dead friend, Jorge

Octavio carried in the street

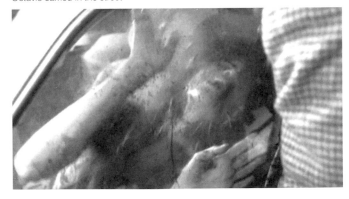

Valeria trapped behind the wheel

performance, changing as she does from brittle model to shattered invalid, the loss of the back story perhaps explains the limited direction of sympathy to her compared with the other characters and her invisibility to some audiences. Given the narrative and visual charge usually carried by youth, beauty and femininity, such apparently minute considerations of narrative help to explain why a grizzled old man such as El Chivo (whose motives are more fully explained) looms larger in the spectator's memory than the superficially more attractive Valeria.

But narrative structure cannot be read independently of national context. How then does *Amores Perros* measure up to previous Mexican cinema and telenovela? In his excellent book *Cinema of Solitude*, Charles Ramírez Berg gives a full account of the New Cinema which coincided with the political and economic crisis that began in the late 1960s. Berg claims that '*mexicanidad* has been the key concept in Mexican intellectual, political, and artistic thought for most of this century'.[16] The quest for an authentically Mexican perspective sought to transcend the divided experience of a nation caught between Old World roots and New World location in an 'extended identity crisis'.[17] Seeking to understand the ideology of classical Mexican cinema Berg examines the lachrymose family melodrama *Cuando los hijos se van/When the Children Leave* (1941). Its essential features are: capitalism; patriarchy; machismo; woman as virgin/Virgin/whore/wife/mother; class; the church; Indians; migration; and history.[18] While all of these elements are taken for granted in classical film, some of them are explicitly present (capitalism, machismo), others are significant absences (the church, Indians), and still others are unattainable ideals (the image of the perfect woman, the nostalgia for a lost historical past).

Berg writes that the internal contradictions of this vast and complex system led it to collapse in the late 1960s, 'because industrial complacency and unimaginative film-making practices ... resulted in a progressively shoddy, creatively stultified cinema'. This 'creative vacuum' coincided with political and ideological collapse.[19] Stepping in to redefine *mexicanidad*, new directors broke down traditional roles by depicting women in revolt and the macho in extremis; paid proper attention to the Indian question;

redefined communities, both personal and political; and rerouted departures: to the city, the North (US) and the past.

González Iñárritu has often said in interview that he is in revolt against the directors who preceded him. It is surprising, then, to see how easily *Amores Perros* fits into the broad framework sketched by Berg. Capitalism is dominant to the extreme in *Amores Perros*, from Octavio's vicious dogfighting, via Valeria's cut-throat world of modelling (she is sacked soon after the accident), to Gustavo's extension of commercial competition to include the execution of one's business rival. Machismo is embodied by Susana's brutal teenage husband, its crisis by Octavio's own more tender, albeit adulterous, wooing of the young bride. While the saintly, sexy and pregnant schoolgirl Susana is virgin/Virgin/whore/wife/mother, Octavio's dried-up and downtrodden mother (where is his father?) plays the part of long-suffering matriarch, albeit without the slightest trace of melodrama. The polarised social registers suggest continuing class conflict, while the close-ups of domestic crucifixes and altars point to the continuing presence of the church, even though no character is shown to attend mass. Indians are, as ever, absent, their trace only in the mestizo features of some of the actors; and the longed-for migration takes the form of Octavio's modest dream of moving to Ciudad Juárez with Susana. Wholly absent from *Amores Perros* is the theme of

Gustavo, yuppie businessman

nostalgia for past plenitude. Indeed the only historical reference reveals the characters' amnesia to national history. When told that El Chivo had once been a leftist guerrilla in the 1970s, yuppie businessman Gustavo asks if he was in the Zapatistas (the indigenous rebels of the 1990s).

There is scarcely an element of *Amores Perros*'s intricate plot, then, that is not anticipated in the crisis of national identity explored in Mexican cinema two decades earlier. What makes González Iñárritu unique, however, is that these elements are not placed within a self-conscious quest for *mexicanidad* but are rather (as García Tsao wrote) subordinated to the attempt to tell a story as effectively as possible.

That narrative dynamic is also clear in a more pervasive and contemporary Mexican medium, the telenovela. Ayala did not mean to praise *Amores Perros* when he compared it to a soap opera. But one aspect of González Iñárritu's daring is the way in which he sails so close to that much despised genre. All three of *Amores Perros*'s episodes could be rewritten for the 'series melodramas' (as telenovelas prefer to be called), featuring as they do impassioned and incestuous forbidden desires. Promotion of the film even played up the similarity, using a variable tag line of emotive abstractions: 'Love is sacrifice, instinct, pain, hope'. In his entertaining book *Sangre de mi sangre* ('Blood of My Blood'), Álvaro Cueva, who proudly claims to be the only specialist in this field to have served both behind and in front of the camera, offers six defining characteristics of the telenovela. These are: nationalism; censure of the rich; class struggle; problems of identity; Third World-ism; and victimism.[20]

We have seen that *Amores Perros*, for all its depiction of national squalor, also served as a focus for Mexican pride. Its critique of the wealthy is shown in the humbling of shallow and successful media types Valeria and Daniel. Typical of telenovelas' version of class struggle, according to Cueva, is that their heroes and heroines do not think of earning their fortune but rather expect to inherit their money through some spectacular, but untaxing, gambit: Octavio's dog fighting and El Chivo's contract killings pass this test. Just as the telenovela is indefinable (preferring to be described as a 'serial' or 'series drama') so *Amores Perros* also defies classification, drawing on at least three genres, one for each episode. The telenovela's Third World-ism lies in the fact that (unlike Protestant US soaps) it prefers to reduce the rich to penury than to raise the poor to honest wealth. Finally its victimism lies in that, contrary to common belief, it fails to provide happy endings but rather condemns its highly coloured inhabitants to failure. One telenovela even ended with the whole cast lost in the wilderness. Just so in *Amores Perros* Octavio's scheme for easy money comes to nought and Valeria's lucrative career is cut short. And in the final image (in the film, not the script), El Chivo disappears into a black desert on the farthest edge of the city.

Now just as *Amores Perros* is not an example of politically committed New Cinema, so it is clearly light years from the typical telenovela. Yet it shares narrative arcs and even ideological values with both genres. One key to *Amores Perros*'s domestic success was the emergence of a new audience, more partial to intelligent and youthful fare from Mexican cinema. Cueva suggests indirectly a more concrete cause for the success of this national narrative. He writes that telenovelas are the 'companions of dictatorship':

It is no accident that series melodramas have kept Mexicans company during the last years, nor is it a coincidence that they should triumph in countries with the worst social problems … Until 2001 at the end of every *sexenio* [six-year Presidential term] there has been a 'smash hit' telenovela, a ratings phenomenon, a story that paralysed whole cities and became legendary, it was so famous and popular.[21]

Hence the current decadence of the genre, which has lost its sense of purpose. In a transition to democracy the telenovelas, with their stubbornly conservative ideology, feel as out of step with the times as the engaged New Cinema, some of which was in thrall to an equally outdated Marxism. Reflected and refracted through the prism of a decadent genre (dubbed by Cueva 'the dictatorship of tears'), *Amores Perros* thus filled that same need for a newly educated and youthful nation at the end of a crucial *sexenio*. But, aided by professional marketing, *Amores Perros* benefited from an international prestige that the soaps, long scorned and mocked for their provincialism, could only dream of.

3 Love Is Sacrifice

OCTAVIO: **Did you know that in Guadalajara when a baby boy is born the doctors put a finger up his arse?**
SUSANA: **What for?**
OCTAVIO: **To find out what his job will be. Look: if he screams, he'll be a mariachi; if he kicks, he'll be a footballer; and if he laughs, he'll be a queer.**
SUSANA: **And if it's a girl, what then?**
OCTAVIO: **They keep fingering her until she turns eighteen.**

The clearest link between the prestigious and celebrated *Amores Perros* and the despised and threatened telenovela is the familiarity of many of its supposedly unknown cast from TV soaps. Cueva's study of the genre even has a still of a fresh-faced Gael García, age twelve, in *El abuelo y yo/Grandfather and Me* (1992), a world away from scrawny, sexy Octavio. (Later García would study for three years at London's Central School of Speech and Drama.) Other graduates of soap school in the cast are Vanessa Bauche (Susana) and Jorge Salinas (Luis). Rodrigo Murray (Gustavo) hosted a real-life chat show, ironic given *Amores Perros*'s merciless parody of television. The telenovela is known, erroneously according to Cueva, as a female genre. Yet in its current guise there is a conflict between traditional romance and more radical realism, as exemplified by the graphic new plot lines of *Agua y aceite*. Perhaps the best known of Latin American soaps for the end of the millennium is the Colombian *Yo soy Betty la fea/I Am Ugly Betty* (1999), dismissively scheduled by the nationalist Mexican Televisa on a Saturday afternoon. Here an unconventional heroine (bad hair, prominent teeth braces and huge spectacles) successfully takes on the company where she starts work as a humble secretary. However crude its characterisation and performance style, *Betty* nonetheless positions women in the workplace and radically revises the look of the female protagonist.

Amores Perros is dedicated in the end credits to Abba and Pater (Hebrew and Latin for 'father'); and all of its women characters are confined to the home and remain dependent on men. In this new context, then, is the film reactionary, even patriarchal? For Berg the New Cinema of the 1970s marked the breakdown of traditional roles whereby men had been mobile and active in the public sphere, women immobile and passive in the private sphere.[22] This cinematic shift corresponded to social changes in Mexico. Formal equality at work and before the law was legislated, if not enforced, in 1974. Meanwhile migration to the city and widespread emigration by men to the US piled the pressure on a growing number of female-headed households. On the other hand, the new access to contraception in the 1970s (not shown to be the case in *Amores Perros*'s underclass) gave rise to a 'sexual revolution'.[23]

Today broken families are so numerous they even include the First Family of the nation: *TVyNovelas* reported, among the star gossip, on the straitened circumstances of the abandoned consort of the ex-President, obliged to look after the children on her own (5 February 2002). In this context *Amores Perros*, with its vision of female sacrifice, seems at first sight to be a throwback to a period even before the the Golden Age of the 1940s which celebrated the *cabaretera* or *fichera* (saloon girl). Previously a Catholic Mexican cinema had, in the words of cultural commentator Carlos Monsiváis, 'exalted the repression of instincts in favour of moral servitude'.[24] This is a strangely regressive tendency for a film which proved ideally suited to a unique moment of change and democratisation in Mexican history.

The three main female characters of *Amores Perros* are named in the intertitles that introduce each episode: Susana, Valeria and Maru. We first see Susana in long shot in the street, dressed in the coy school uniform that includes white ankle socks. This will be one of the few shots of her outside the home. Indeed even here her role is as (failed) guardian of the hearth: when she opens the door her husband Ramiro's dog Cofi makes a break for freedom. Once inside the house Susana's first lines of dialogue establish her conflict between schooling and childcare. Addressing her mother-in-law formally as 'señora' she asks in vain for her baby to be taken care of as she has an exam coming up. Female solidarity is absent here. 'I raised my children: now you raise yours' is the curt response. Susana can

Simple Susana

Vain Valeria

Mute Maru

expect no help either from her own mother who, dazed by alcohol, neglects the child.

On the other hand, the opening scenes show a growing complicity between Susana and her brother-in-law Octavio, who takes the blame for the dog's disappearance. After a first vicious dogfighting scene, González Iñárritu cuts straight to a sizzling pan of meat and veg: Octavio's mother is preparing lunch. In the crowded kitchen (sickly yellow tiles on the walls, a too small table laden with objects), Susana balances the baby on her lap. She looks up smiling as Octavio comes in and sits opposite her. The previously jittery camera stops to pay attention and the couple are held in two-shot for some thirty seconds, a clear sign that this relationship between brother and sister-in-law will be central to the story. As the bantering dialogue continues, the camera moves closer to observe Susana's soft, round face, flooded with light from the window. As so often in *Amores Perros*, the narrative force and emotional charge are carried not by the profanity-spattered dialogue, but by the pregnant looks of the young actors. Susana may turn up her nose at Octavio's smutty jokes, but her eyes say otherwise.

Bitter sibling rivalry between Octavio and Ramiro sets up Susana as an alibi for intense emotions between men. Heterosexual relations, meanwhile, are far from reciprocal. Ramiro tears Susana's ear by pulling her earring, a hint at more brutal cruelties. Even his gifts are double-edged. Returning late at night from a robbery, Ramiro wakes Susana to give her a Walkman: she can clearly hear the music (Illya Kuryaki's raucous 'Coolo'), but he and we cannot. In spite of her protests he also wakes the sickly baby, whom Susana has taken so long to nurse to sleep. Male support is absent where it is needed (Ramiro refuses to buy nappies for his child or food for his mother to cook with) and excessive where it is given, unasked (Susana needs not a Walkman but childcare). Even Octavio's deep felt love is presented in such a way as to qualify its disinterestedness. The younger brother buys the baby things the older brother ('natural' father) neglects. But Octavio's motive can also be seen as paternalistic: appropriating the baby and even Susana's second, unborn child. (Abortion and contraception are not shown as an option for the working class.)

Gravely he lays his hand on her belly, attempting to persuade her to run off with him.

The first time Octavio and Susana make love is clearly signalled as a significant moment in the film: it is also the first time in which Gustavo Santaolalla's expert score makes an appearance, after half an hour without backing music. It is a love theme which will recur when wealthy Daniel and Valeria embrace also. However, there is always something that intrudes between Octavio and Susana when they make love: the first time the baby lies on the bed beside them; on the second occasion Octavio gazes fiercely at his own face in the cracked bedroom mirror, as if to reassure himself of the reality of his desire. This sex scene is part of a rhythmic montage, crosscut with Ramiro working (and fucking a co-worker) at the supermarket and the bloody dogfighting contests. And it is set not to the romantic guitar chord but rather to hard Mexican rap from Control Machete: the chanted refrain goes 'Tell me you can feel the sweat on your brow'. The labour of love is compared and contrasted with the vicious exploitation of employment, both legal and illegal. Sound and image track serve, then, to bracket and qualify our experience of the young couple's affair even as the narrative encourages us to identify with them and cheer them on. In spite of the confinement of women to the home, the couple cannot be isolated from society. Private and public interpenetrate and will come into violent conflict.

There remains an imbalance, however. The dogfighting is a wholly masculine arena for a vicarious battle of virility which is scarcely veiled. And it leads Octavio into three city locations, variously permeable to the outside world: the inner room of Mauricio (the master of the fights), his rooftop terrace (we glimpse the low-rise *colonia* and a church tower), and the abandoned luxury house where the climactic fight takes place in a disused swimming pool. Susana, stuck at home, has no more access to these locations than she does to the pharmacies held up by her husband Ramiro. Content, or so it appears, to see the money pile up in the 'bank' she keeps with Octavio in an old box hidden in the cupboard, she shows no aspirations to accumulate capital herself. Unconvinced as to the propriety of infidelity (even when brutalised by her husband), Susana is left at the end repressing her instincts in favour of moral servitude: she refuses to join Octavio after Ramiro's death and will even name her unborn child after his abusive father. But if she appears willingly to take on the role of La Llorona (the archetypal Mexican weeping woman) or even Antigone (the classical mourner who stays loyal to the dead male), then we have been clearly shown the causes of her conundrum. Poverty, lack of education and, crucially, absence of contraception (with abortion a hot topic in Mexico at the time of writing) have left her no choice.

Model Valeria, on the other hand, has all the aces. Young, rich and beautiful, she is (as viewers in Guadalajara remarked) a case study for the vanity and banality of female beauty. A dead ringer for the many blonde celebrities on talk shows such as *Hoy/Today* (ribbed in the film as *Gente de hoy/People Today*) and in the ubiquitous gossip magazines like *TVyNovelas*, Valeria's tall and willowy body, proudly displayed over several floors of apartment block, could hardly be further from the small, dark and vulnerable Susana, confined in a claustrophobic working-class home. In the second episode, moreover, there is a shift from the poverty and cruelty (but also danger and excitement) of Octavio's swift-moving masculine world to the falsity and superficiality of a fetishised mass media that is coded as feminine. Larger than life in the huge poster that confronts her new flat (given to her without her knowledge by boyfriend Daniel), Valeria is truly spectacular: the Mexican Spanish for 'billboard' is, significantly enough, 'espectacular'. Elevated (and burdened) by the ambivalent charge of visibility, Valeria is the perfect mate for Daniel, who is also held hostage by the cult of the image. A middle-aged man with a suspiciously regular hairline (wig or transplant?), Daniel works at a glossy magazine and, like Valeria, prostitutes himself to the reproductive image. Andrés, the male star who pretends to be Valeria's boyfriend on TV, is rewarded with the cover of Daniel's latest issue: we watch the staff manipulate his handsome face on the computer screen. In the age of universal media coverage (which penetrates even Octavio's squalid bedroom), the narcissism of the feminine masquerade is clearly no longer confined to women. Two scenes in the script that were excluded from the final cut make this explicit. As sex symbol Andrés waits with Daniel at the hospital for news of Valeria he is approached by an intrusive female fan and accosted by the news media, avid for details of personal tragedy.

A working woman, Valeria is plainly set up (in all senses) as superficial, ripe for a fall. Unable to cook (Daniel takes care of their celebratory lunch), she seems barely able to eat, with her trademark model's emaciated frame. Insecure on strappy high heels in her short pistachio sundress, and clutching her annoying white poodle, Valeria trips over the hole in the parquet floor, the most transparent prefiguration of her fall from grace. Yet the car crash will reveal what we had surely guessed before: that Valeria's body is not all surface (glossy page or poster), that even she has hidden depths. González Iñárritu gives us merciless close-ups of the jagged stitches that deform her leg and the cumbersome brace which turns her into a kind of cyborg, half woman, half machine. The fashion system is thoroughly demystified. Valeria may flick through magazines at home, but she is swiftly dumped as a cripple by her employers, the ironically named fragrance 'Enchant'. Stripped of make-up, she lingers longingly on a different kind of photo: the unposed snapshots of her as a child (a back story to which the viewer is consistently denied access). As Octavio confronts himself in the mirror even at the most intimate of moments, so Valeria, in extremis, takes solace in images of herself that imply both likeness and difference, identification and alienation.

Andrés on the computer

Crucial here is her foreignness, which enhances her isolation. Although skilled in Mexican profanity, Valeria keeps the Spanish accent and much of the distinctive vocabulary of actress Goya Toledo, who hails from the Canaries. Answering the phone (a key prop in *Amores Perros*) she, uniquely in the film, uses a European '¿Diga?' rather than a Mexican '¿Bueno?'. Deprived of the psychological depth granted by knowledge of her personal history, Valeria is confined not just to the small space of a sterile apartment but to the present time with all its mounting horrors of defacement, loneliness and disability. The only clue we have to her past is that she refuses to inform her Spanish family of the accident, commenting that her father would be capable of saying his (adulterous) daughter deserved her fate. As throughout the film, here there is a crisis in patriarchy: the father is always lacking. But while Octavio and Susana's lack of a father goes unexplained, Daniel's separation from his wife and daughters reveals the psychic cost of family breakdown, for men as for women. The unanswered phones that ring throughout this episode speak silently of a radical rupture in communication between the sexes.

The apparent denunciation of the rich here is, however, quite different to the leftism of some New Cinema or the populism of the telenovela. Daring to show sympathy for the devil, González Iñárritu explicitly parallels proletariat and bourgeoisie. Valeria may never meet

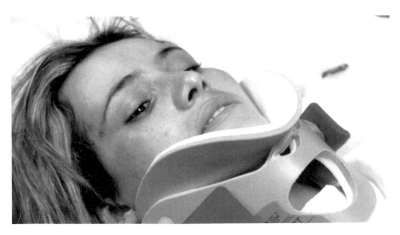

Valeria as cyborg

Susana, but when each woman embraces their adulterous lover the same love theme plays, tender and ominous, on the soundtrack. And the second episode, so different in social setting, shares yet more with the first than might appear. Valeria (in the script at least) has the abortion that Susana will not, and her poodle is a pathetic substitute for a child. But both women share a problem in filiation: the father's line is disrupted. Moreover both are left worse off than they began. Susana has lost a husband, however brutal, and a friend, however self-interested. Valeria has lost her lucrative, albeit trivial, career. If image is alienating, then lack of image is social death: the empty hoarding where her poster once stood is 'available', but Valeria herself is not.

But just as Susana stays true to her dead husband, so Daniel remains faithful to his mutilated lover (to the end of the episode at least) in the private space of their new and fateful home. Episode three, however, returns to the male sphere of public life. Here sibling rivalry is deadly once more as business practice extends to contract killing: Gustavo hires El Chivo to take out the half-brother who is cheating him at work, or so he claims. The nominal female focus here (Maru) is yet more attenuated than in the previous episodes. Deserted long ago by her father, El Chivo, she is only to be looked at: he stations himself outside her plush home to observe her as she leaves in a protective four-wheel drive. Indeed we never hear Maru speak except through the perky message on her answerphone. As in the previous episodes, this father is fragile, easily replaced by a stepfather, when El Chivo is sent to prison for his terrorist attacks. With long hair and matted beard, Emilio Echevarría (who later appeared in Nicolás Echevarría's *Vivir mata*) looks like a biblical patriarch, an effect enhanced by his references to Cain and Abel. Avenging but loving, El Chivo is the most extreme example of failed reciprocity with women. After the failure of his revolutionary ambitions, he agrees with his wife that daughter Maru should be told he is dead. Like Valeria, he attempts to construct a biography through family photos. But in his case it can be only through the fragmentary medium of collage: he sticks his own image over the face of the stepfather in the formal photo celebrating Maru's university graduation. The lack of fit is obvious.

Moreover the father's confession is mediated by technology: the phone that also plays such a role in the second episode. Although El Chivo is physically present in his absent daughter's bedroom he leaves a tearful message on her machine, revealing the truth of his disappearance and teaching her (and himself?) a lesson in love. However, if this is, once more, a final example of fidelity, such as we find at the end of the first two episodes, it remains unsatisfying. Fathers are absent throughout *Amores Perros* and women obliged to take their place (Maru is protected by her unsympathetic aunt). Relations between the sexes are thus at best illusory (El Chivo will never know what it would have been like to have had daily contact with his daughter) and the most dramatically potent and spectacularly visible affairs are those between men. Maru leaves silently in her SUV and does not confront the man she cannot recognise as her father. The two half-brothers, tied and tricked by El Chivo, snarl at each other like dogs, the very image of feral conflict. It is not difficult to decide which attracts more attention from the camera and the audience.

But it would be naive to think that *Amores Perros* is in favour of the sex and gender relations it depicts. And if its representation of women and men seems reactionary, especially given the social changes that have occurred in recent decades in Mexico, then unlike earlier melodrama it shows what happens not 'when the children go', but rather when the fathers go, or when no children come at all. Tensions within the family are replaced by conflicts between the couple, whether adulterous lovers or estranged parent and child. In *Amores Perros* there is a female lineage, however constrained and confused: Susana will care for her child alone, as Maru's mother continued to do also after the loss of her husband, albeit in very different circumstances. The men have less success: Ramiro is dead and his brother Octavio isolated; Daniel is cast out from the family home and El Chivo lost in the wasteland with his dog. In the extreme space of the city, the final moral may be the Christian one shared by the telenovelas: that suffering brings salvation to those who turn the other cheek.[25]

4 Seismic City

VALERIA: **This sofa is identical to the one in my house.**

ANDRÉS: **It's not identical: it *is* the one in your house; and if you go to the bedroom you'll find your clothes, your perfumes.**

VALERIA: **What are you playing at, you bastard?**

ANDRÉS: **That's not all: look what a pretty view you have.**

[Andrés gestures towards the poster of Valeria on the building opposite.]

VALERIA: **You're frightening me.**

ANDRÉS: **Here you are: this is the key to your apartment.**

VALERIA: **My apartment?**

DANIEL **[offscreen]: Our apartment.**

Many critics have claimed that *Amores Perros* shows us a Mexico City never seen before on film. In the Cannes pressbook (as repeatedly in interview) González Iñárritu himself states:

Mexico City is an anthropological experiment, and I feel I'm part of it. I'm just one of the twenty-one million people in the world's largest and most populated city. In the past, no person had ever lived (survived, more likely) in a city with

'You're frightening me'

such rates of pollution, violence, and corruption; however – incredible and
paradoxical as it may seem – it is a beautiful, fascinating city, and that is
precisely what *Amores Perros* is to me: a product of this contradiction, a small
reflection of the baroque and complex mosaic that is Mexico City.[26]

The shoot itself, made entirely on location, was occasionally perilous: the
small crew was challenged by armed youths when attempting to film the
final dogfight. Emilio Echevarría lived for an extended period with the
sometimes dangerous dogs, growing hair, beard and nails, and spending
real life in the startling guise of El Chivo. For González Iñárritu, as for
some of his colleagues, it would seem that the city and cinema are one.

But just as the 'newness' of *Amores Perros* hides traditional gender
roles, so the supposed immediacy of its depiction of the city (which is lived
rather than represented) conceals curious contradictions. It is hardly
surprising that *Amores Perros* avoids tourist shots of the Zócalo and the
Historic Centre. But it also neglects the soaring and sometimes distinctive
skyscrapers of the several business districts. This is curious, because the
combination of ancient and modern is (uniquely for an American capital),
the distinctive characteristic of Mexico City where delapidated sixteenth-
century chapels can rub shoulders with gleaming glass towers.

Moreover there is barely one recognisable building depicted in the
153 minutes running time. The contrast with a recent production such
as *Vivir mata* is telling. The latter features frequent aerial shots and
prominent landmarks as diverse as the soaring 'Angel' monument on the
grand thoroughfare Paseo de la Reforma, the glamorous white marble
Palacio de Bellas Artes (where *Amores Perros* won its many Ariel awards),
and the huge sculptured head of Juárez made by muralist Siqueiros.
Further comparison with *Vivir mata* (a much inferior version of the
metropolis in spite of the loving attention it devotes to urban architecture)
suggests a more surprising absence. If there are no grand monuments, nor
are we shown the spontaneous street activities equally typical of the city:
the vendors and eccentrically varied performers who entertain the
motorists in traffic jams and at stop lights. González Iñárritu avoids both
urban stereotypes of touristic glamour and ethnographic local colour.

Watching the film, however, the audience is never aware of these absences and simply takes *Amores Perros*'s unique vision of extreme urbanism on its own terms.

The poor neighbourhoods shown in *Amores Perros* are by no means the setting for a rich sociality like that of the nineteenth-century metropolis. Octavio's *colonia* is no East End or Lower East Side and in keeping with the low-rise, relatively low-density architecture, there are no crowded pavements in the barrio. The film's urban areas, both rich and poor, are generic and the locations in which they were shot difficult to pinpoint even for locals. Press reports name Octavio's neighbourhood as Santa Fe; the documentation made when scouting locations shows otherwise. While this confusion corresponds to the polycentric nature of the megalopolis, with its huge number of relatively autonomous *colonias*, the spatial disorientation experienced in watching the film is clearly deliberate. On the ground the grand boulevards known as 'axes' do provide some sort of abstract grid for 'reading' the city's neighbourhoods in relation to one another. Of course film space is not city space: directors have no obligation to replicate the actual layout of streets. Nonetheless it is telling that the film mentions only two streets by name (the work and home addresses of El Chivo's victim Luis), and these serve as a simple index of social class: 'Some proletarian', remarks the grizzled killer ironically on hearing the street names. The script is equally imprecise, confirming only that Valeria's new apartment lies in the notoriously yuppie central *colonia* of Condesa, just south-east of the Chapultepec park. González Iñárritu does not rely on local references and ensures that audiences unfamiliar with Mexico City do not feel excluded from his film.

The first sound in *Amores Perros* is a distorted whoosh of moving cars. The first shot is of blurred white lines in the middle of the road. The second shot shows Octavio and friend Jorge in their beaten-up car. For a split second there is a glimpse in the distance, shaky and blurred, of the Latin American Tower with its distinctive spire. Proclaimed by its owners to be a 'symbol of Mexico City', the tower, at the intersection of the major avenues named for the presidents Juárez and Lázaro Cárdenas, is a steel and glass pastiche of the Manhattan masonry skyscrapers built some twenty years earlier. The tower was completed in 1956 and has survived earthquakes ever since. The French journal *Positif* reads the distorted sound which plays over this sequence as volcanic or seismic, proof that the earth shifts beneath the city's surface.[27] More evident perhaps is the contrast set up here from the very beginning between speed and space, motion and location. This tension will be kept up throughout the film.

However, if there is no time like the present (the visceral pull of the car chase, the erasure of history from an ancient city), there is no place like home. The many domestic interiors both define the class positions of the characters and point towards their state of mind. The two-storey house of Octavio's family (not a flat, as some critics state) is dense, crowded and visually differentiated from room to room. Octavio's bedroom, where he smokes, broods and watches TV, is mainly blue; Ramiro and Susana's, scene of sex and violence, is red. González Iñárritu often starts a domestic sequence with an extreme close-up of a prop: the rotating mobile on Susana's ceiling or crawling baby toy by her bed. Octavio's mother is imaged rather in a homely altar on the stairs, featuring a chocolate-box Christ and a plaster Virgin.

González Iñárritu cuts for graphic contrast from this claustrophobic working-class interior to the more ample spaces of Daniel's family home. When Daniel takes a surreptitious phone call from Valeria, the corridor

Susana's crawling baby toy

stretches behind him into the distance. Unlike Octavio and Susana, Daniel and his wife are shown in long shot, emphasising the size of their bedroom and the length of their (unhappy) married bed. But an iconographic link is made with Octavio's cramped and distant home: a large crucifix hangs on the wall above the adulterous husband. A further graphic match, this time bitterly ironic, establishes a connection between El Chivo's decrepit compound and his daughter Maru's luxury home:

Daniel's crucifix

Maru's gates

both are protected by metal gates. While El Chivo's gates are scarred and spotted with ironic political stickers recalling past elections, Maru's fortress-like entrance is more aesthetic, typical of wealthy neighbourhoods such as the southern suburb of El Pedregal. Both serve a function at once social and psychological: to keep out the horror of the city beyond.

It is Valeria's story, shot almost entirely within her sterile new flat, which reveals that the domestic womb can also be a tomb. The viewer sees the flat for the first time when Valeria does. She and Andrés come into a plain, provisional space, with smooth pastel walls and packing cases. Valeria lowers Richi from her protective arm to the pale wooden floor. The camera rotates to follow the elegantly dressed pair as they walk to the French windows that open on to a balcony. There is a glimpse of a white sofa, glass coffee table and bent-wood chairs. Valeria, wary at discovering her furniture in a strange new space, looks out of the window at her own image on the poster. Her face is, just for a second, bleached white by the light. It is an ominous hint that domesticity can be dangerous. Even this place, so cool and calm, cannot resist the dangers of the city beyond the balcony.

Private space, controlled and strictly delimited, is always under threat from outside. Daniel's office, cold glass cubicles devoid of domestic comfort, is typical of a rigorously zoned workplace. (The location is actually that of González Iñárritu's own production company, Zeta.) But for most characters home and work cannot be separated. Fat Mauricio runs the lucrative dogfighting business from his home (kennels are on the roof) and he takes his family meals not far from the bloody residue of battle. El Chivo's derelict and desolate living space, packed with rubbish (what is the purpose of the piles of newspapers?), also doubles as a killing field. He plans his hits and even confines his final victims there. Television brings alien locations into Octavio's humble room, notably the talk show whose set mimics a bourgeois interior. The telephone disrupts Daniel's dreams of domesticity, even in the hard-won new home which he proudly introduces to Valeria as 'our apartment' and has secretly filled with her favourite things. Ironically, once more, the most intimate events are displayed most publicly: Valeria's mutilation in the street and Ramiro's dead body in the funeral home are both exposed to strangers.

Architectural features either promote or prevent the separation of urban spaces. The glamorous flats and offices of Condesa are approached or exited by protective flights of stairs. Octavio's house, on the other hand, opens straight on to the street (hence Cofi's first and fatal escape). The spectacle of the city leads the wealthy to put themselves on display even as they also seek to hide themselves from the poor. El Chivo's first victim is shot through the plate-glass window of a Japanese restaurant (the blood sizzles on the hot plate); his second lunches with his adulterous girlfriend in full view of the street (he is saved when El Chivo is distracted by the car crash). Liminal or threshold spaces are barely contained by semi-permeable boundaries such as windows. The camera often spies on actors inside buildings: El Chivo is shown behind his window (whose point of view can this be?), as is Ramiro when he robs the first pharmacy (the carnage is seen but not heard). Graphic matches link across the episodes once more suggesting a deadly confusion between inside and outside. Both Octavio and Valeria are marked by shadows of Venetian blinds, domestic versions of prison bars. The seismic city of Mexico is not safe even below: just beneath Valeria's smooth parquet floor is that unsuspected place of horror and disgust where Richi cowers and rats roam. The earth moves beneath even the most elegantly shod feet.

For the nineteenth-century *flâneur* the street was a site of encounter (and vicious El Jarocho will come across Cofi by accident in just such a way). More typically, however, *Amores Perros* shows not the street as a site for social intercourse but the road as a conduit for anonymous traffic. El Chivo is first glimpsed behind the blurred and roaring forms of speeding cars; and twice there are night shots of endless headlights glittering white on damp tarmac. González Iñárritu chooses to show no trace of the very particular and popular public transport in D.F.: the excellent metro, handy *peseros* (buses which stop on request) and distinctive green Volkswagen taxis. Characters are confined to private cars, which are in the city, but not of it. Daniel's family bicker as if at home, while he looks up from the steering wheel to see his secret lover on the poster. Businessman Gustavo cruises at speed with bent cop Leonardo, but his shiny Mercedes and cellular phone (symbols of effortless mobility) will not stop him being tied firmly to a post by El Chivo. The pivotal car crash shows that, however segregated social classes may be through urban zoning and income differential, they cannot be hermetically insulated from one another: people will touch each other, often with fatal results.

In the final scene El Chivo sells his car to a scrap dealer and sets out on foot with his dog into a black wilderness on the edge of the city. As he walks away from us into the distance, this is the only time the horizon is seen in the film. It is an ominously flat landscape, typical of Mexico's high central valley, with characteristic volcanic hills in the distance. Geological or tectonic in nature, this setting lies beyond human habitation, which is revealed by default as the unique possibility for love. This is a symbolic and sacrificial landscape from which the father will perhaps return, purified, to his beloved daughter. But the newly open space suggests a defiantly open ending: as the credits roll, the audience cannot be sure what will happen next.

One fascinating testimony to the elaboration of *Amores Perros*'s urban vision is a large-format scrapbook held in the offices of production company Altavista. The book was used during pre-production both to develop the broad visual style of the film through found images and, more concretely, to document locations that had been scouted. This archive source confirms the actual locations where scenes were shot (the crash was

El Chivo in the wilderness

on the corner of Atlixco and Juan Escutia, in genteel Condesa once more; Octavio's house was in distant San Andrés Tetepilco) and the evidence it provides of how poor people actually live in Mexico City is pathetic in the extreme. Architectural plans of each dwelling made specially for the shoot also confirm how important domestic space is to each story.

The scrapbook shows how González Iñárritu and his team created a cinematic city which transcends the real. For example, snapshots of the actual locations are preceded by photo collages taken from anonymous magazines or well-known photographers (Nan Goldin, Richard Billingham) that were used to help define what the scrapbook calls 'the world' of each character. Interestingly these materials are international, juxtaposing US and UK materials with the Mexican. The scrapbook also begins to articulate the future editing strategy of *Amores Perros*, which will be based on graphic contrast: juxtaposed on the page are the sordid, crowded dump where El Chivo sells his stolen car and the discreet restaurant (whose real name, significantly enough, is 'Another World') where Luis meets his workplace lover. As García Tsao wrote so perceptively in his Cannes report, all elements here are subordinate to narrative. The real cartography of the city takes second place to the more potent fictional geography re-created in and through the film.

González Iñárritu has said that production designer Brigitte Broch, a German native resident for many years in D.F., still sees things in the city to which Mexicans themselves are blind.[28] In a rather similar way *Amores Perros* achieves a prodigious and shocking effect of the real by making strange what is taken for granted and making us all see the city as if for the first time.

5 A Two-hour Shout?

Dime que se siente	Tell me you can feel
Dime que se siente	Tell me you can feel
Dime que se siente	Tell me you can feel
El sudor en la frente	The sweat on your brow

Dime que se siente	Tell me you can feel
Dime que presientes	Tell me that you'll feel
Dime que se siente	Tell me you can feel
El sudor en la frente	The sweat on your brow

Control Machete, 'Sí, señor'

In the opening interview of the 'Behind the Scenes' documentary extra on the DVD of *Amores Perros*, director Alejandro González Iñárritu begins by saying that if there is one word that sums up the film it is 'visceral'. He goes on to describe the film as 'a shout [or "scream": Spanish *grito*] that lasts for two hours'. First-time viewers, overwhelmed, will be inclined to agree. After all, what could be more graphic than the trail of blood left by the dead dogs as they are dragged from the arena? What more instinctive than Control Machete's rap on that other bodily fluid, sweat? But while González Iñárritu gives a good account of the accumulated emotional power of the film (which resists repeated viewings without losing its effect), his description hardly scratches the surface of *Amores Perros*'s complex and subtle sound and image tracks.

Critical responses to the film varied widely, often according to national debates on the nature of film and censorship. Journalists in the UK focused almost exclusively on the alleged content of *Amores Perros*, that is the brutal dogfights which actually take up around two minutes of the 153 minutes' running time. In 'Dogfight looms on showing feted film' the London *Guardian* wrote (20 February 2001) that 'the strict provisions of the Cinematograph Films (Animals) Act, 1937, means British distributors have been very slow about picking it up despite its triumph at the Edinburgh film festival'. The British Board of Film Classification were quoted as saying that

Our only problem is with one very short scene and the reason we are taking so long to decide is that we can see its importance to the film. Let's be very clear, it is not the Board that is the obstacle here, it is the law, and the law says animals should not be goaded or in any way incited to fight.

González Iñárritu was cited as saying in *Amores Perros*'s defence that 'the camera lies': 'We used hand-held cameras to make it look a lot more dramatic. The dogs were just playing.' A scene included in the 'Behind the Scenes' documentary confirms this claim: two dogs lunge at each other in apparent anger, only to engage at once in vigorous sex.

Even the normally sober *Variety* wrote, exaggerating the visceral violence of the film, that *Amores Perros*'s

main liability to attracting international audiences is the number of scenes in which dogs are injured or killed; though an end-credit disclaimer assures the viewer that no animals were harmed, numerous graphic dog-fight scenes during the film will be difficult for animal lovers. In some countries, censors may even step in to curtail these sequences.[29]

In France things were different. *Le Monde* began its review with an evocation of the spectator's experience of the opening car chase in terms of its acoustic and visual elements:

Screams of fear, screams of tyres, cries of excitement and distress, blood, gunshots, shock. Followed by a 4 x 4 of devilish yellow, the two teenagers' car is smashed into at high speed. Bodies, more blood, more cries, splinters of glass everywhere, sirens spilling over the soundtrack. The opening of the film is like electroshock treatment, masterfully made to shake the audience. The result is guaranteed.[30]

Here we have not only a sensitive response to the experience of seeing and hearing the film; we also have an awareness, from the beginning, that the visceral charge is carefully orchestrated to affect the audience in a specific way. The 'surprise' for the reviewer is not the supposed reality of the dogfights (barely mentioned in the lengthy notice), but the artistry of the director:

González Iñárritu surprises us by not being content with turning narrated stories into images. In the heart of the narratives we can make out an unexpected elegance, which might be thought 'superfluous' to narrative requirements, but which lends the whole film an improbable beauty and is the mark of a true filmmaker. This is the case when the camera lingers on an empty street, a pile of scrap iron, [and] the face of a young woman marked by physical love and the fear of hunger, of solitude, and shame, as the cooking simmers and sizzles … It is difficult to tell to what extent the director is in control of this tremor, this excess. This disturbance [French *trouble*] takes the film, as it were, out of itself.

For British journalists *Amores Perros* is pure content and the only debate concerns how far the trace of the real on celluloid corresponds to the physical actions on set. For their French counterparts, however, cinema is the art of sensation and *Amores Perros* bears witness to an unstable aesthetic excess which goes beyond what is required to tell a story and even the conscious ambitions of the director. González Iñárritu, in contradictory remarks dictated by the context in which they are given

The face of a young woman

(DVD promotion, censorship defence), repeats this paradox. On the one hand the film is a purely visceral cry; on the other it is the crafted product of a lying camera. *Amores Perros* combines the graphic immediacy of Hollywood with the self-conscious artifice of the art movie. This is one secret of its success for an unusually wide range of audiences.

González Iñárritu does not seem to make another obvious defence of the dogfighting scenes, namely that their visceral effect comes as much from the harrowing soundtrack as from the blurred and indistinct images. And a case could be made for the primacy of sound over vision in *Amores Perros*. González Iñárritu told Jonathan Romney, the first of the few British journalists to write sympathetically about the film, of his training as a radio DJ on Mexico City's WFM rock station where he had a daily show: 'Telling stories to people, trying to keep them entertained for three hours. That was my training as a storyteller. You create stories with music, you create soundtracks for the lives of the people in the city – four million listeners every day.'[31] If all elements of the film are subordinate to narrative, then sound simply *is* storytelling for the acoustically sensitive González Iñárritu.

Moreover *Amores Perros* has a minutely crafted soundtrack, credited to sound designer Martín Hernández, which merits listening to in its own right without the distraction of cinematographer Rodrigo Prieto's expert visuals. While the soundtrack can be fully experienced only at a state of the art multiplex, it is hinted at by the 5.1 Dolby digital sound of the DVD with its six separate channels. Michel Chion, the most prolific of writers on the relatively neglected theme of sound in cinema, has discussed the changes introduced by the Dolby sound from the 1980s and exploited to the full by *Amores Perros*:

Dolby ... focuses finer attention on vocal texture, subtle variations of timbre, vibration of vocal cords, resonances. Multitrack sound helps to situate the voice in a more precise relation to other sounds that may be spread out in various directions in space ... Filmmakers can now bring sounds into play *with one another* to define cinematic space, whereas formerly their principal engagement ... had to occur in the interplay between the low-fi monophonic soundtrack and the screen ... The screen is dispossessed.[32]

We need not go as far as Chion, who argues that the image is now relegated to secondary status by the mobile and seductive sounds which transcend the fixed boundaries of the screen. But in a rather similar way *Amores Perros* combines the basic elements of sound (speech, noise and music) into an intricate mix so as to rearticulate cinematic space and time. González Iñárritu exploits in an acoustic register the patterns, symmetries and repetitions also to be found in Guillermo Arriaga's highly crafted script.

If repetition serves to produce resonance, irony and pathos, the test case will be the one event in the film that recurs four times from different perspectives: the car chase and crash. How does the use of sound vary from one version to another? The first sequence, at the very start of the film, highlights the noises noted by *Le Monde*: the whoosh of the car (heard over a black screen before we see the first image), the squealing brakes and car horns, punctuated by isolated gunshots. The boys' rapid-fire overlapping dialogue is peppered by profanity and exclamations. When the crash occurs, a car horn (whose?) sounds continuously as we fade to black. The second version, some 50 minutes later, is quite different, although it is still seen from the boys' point of view. While the same shots are used, albeit abbreviated, the sound design is dominated by an inexplicable (and unsourced) expressionist drone, as if of revolving machinery. The dialogue is also distorted as if through a car radio, as are the brief and jagged fragments of blaring rap music which play over isolated images, apparently at random. Sound is used here subjectively to convey the state of mind of the protagonists, the confused, terrified and exhilarated Octavio and Jorge. But it also serves to implicate the spectator in dramatic irony that at once objectively distances us from the scene (the soundtrack is no longer naturalistic) and subjectively promotes our identification (by this stage of the film we have been drawn into the characters' minds). The distorted sound suggests that we may put ourselves in Octavio's place, but only now that we know the tragic consequences his actions will have.

The third version of the crash occurs just five minutes later. In Valeria's new flat an irritatingly catchy pop song starts to play (unsourced) low in the mix. When she sets out in search of wine with Richi, the sound comes up on the radio as she drives her car. Richi joins in with some spirited yapping. González Iñárritu observes 'fidelity' to the sound source in the driving sequence. He crosscuts several times in and out of the car as Valeria drives past El Chivo pushing his cart in the street and stops at the traffic lights (we glimpse Valeria through the windscreen). The song changes in volume and tonal quality each time we switch from inside to outside, its mindlessly sunny lyrics (so appropriate to that happy day) repeated over and over: 'Sweetheart, my sweetheart, I love you, my sweetheart'. Crash and fade to black. The use of a soundbridge (the song begins, non-naturalistically, before Valeria gets to her car) suggests a continuity of mood between the new apartment and Valeria's festive errand. It is a potentially ambiguous technique, like the subjective use of sound, that is increasingly exploited in the second and third episodes of the film.

Finally, some 40 minutes of screen time later, we see the crash from El Chivo's perspective. Here the play of different acoustic elements is at its most complex. As El Chivo stalks his prey, the adulterous Luis and his girlfriend, in the upmarket streets of Condesa we hear for the first time a new version of Gustavo Santaolalla's original soundtrack theme, here renamed 'Chivo Groove'. The familiar romantic guitar cord is now treated

Valeria drives her car

with a much heavier and more ominous reverb and supplemented by a
rock steady beat and drum machine. As the killer follows his victim down
the street a dog howls (where? whose?), to be taken up by a squealing sax.
Inexplicably in this smart setting there is a fragment of mariachi music (it
will recur, also unsourced, when Octavio waits in vain at the bus station).
This sequence of fluid travelling shots is sewn together by continuous
music playing for some four minutes, an unprecedented length in the film
so far. We hear the briefest snatch of the yapping Richi as Valeria cruises
by. El Chivo takes up his position outside the restaurant, ready for the hit.
With the sudden (but now anticipated) crash in the street behind him,
the music comes to an abrupt end, giving way to pure ambient sound:
Octavio's screams as he is carried from the car, ambulance sirens drawing
closer, Valeria's desperate pleas. In an acoustic match, implying continuity
once more, sirens, more distant now, play over the next shot in which El
Chivo wheels the wounded Cofi home to his grimy compound.

The widely different sonic landscapes González Iñárritu (or Martín
Hernández) elaborates for each successive version of the car crash are not
simply for the purpose of elegant variation. They are also typical of some
general strategies in the film that only become audible on closer hearing.
The first is that, contradicting *Amores Perros*'s supposed excess of both
style and content, González Iñárritu exploits economy of means wherever
possible. Apart from brief snatches of music low in the mix when gangster
El Jarocho stalks the street or fights his unlucky dogs and when Susana
listens to her new and unwelcome Walkman, there is no music in the film
(not even over the opening credits) until the first montage sequence 36
minutes in. Here Control Machete's pounding rap plays over a
rhythmically edited succession of disparate images: Octavio and Jorge at
the dogfight; Octavio and Susana counting money at home; Octavio
buying his car from a salesman; Ramiro robbing a pharmacy, screwing his
colleague at work, and tensely taking breakfast with Octavio and Susana
at home. Delaying gratification even longer, Gustavo Santaolalla's original
soundtrack is not heard until 41 minutes have passed. The tender five-
note love theme known simply as 'Tema Amores Perros' sounds only
when, scared, excited and ashamed, Susana allows Octavio to make love

to her for the first time. Even here, at such a vital plot point, González Iñárritu uses a soundbridge. With the theme still playing, we cut to a whirring blur of gold and purple, revealed in a wide shot to be the night light of Daniel's daughters. As he kisses them goodnight for the very last time, paternal love is acoustically equated with adulterous and semi-incestuous passion. Both the teenage dogfighter and the middle-aged executive will lose the thing they most love.

Typically, then, González Iñárritu is reticent about the introduction of acoustic elements, pacing the audience through the lengthy running time. But his manipulation of sound becomes increasingly complex as *Amores Perros* develops. Thus all of the sound in the first third of the film (until the irruption of 'Sí, señor' with the montage) is 'diegetic' or sourced within the story space. This does not preclude delicate sound effects: traffic noise and dog barking are interwoven in many different contexts to create a shifting but consistent urban soundscape. Soundbridges pick up the pace, using acoustic overlap to weave together distinct locations. The phone rings as Daniel looks up from the family car at the poster of Valeria; his wife picks it up at home in the next shot. Sound is itself thematised early on, turned into part of the plot: when Daniel takes Valeria's phone call in bed his wife complains she cannot hear the television, thus giving him an excuse to leave the unhappy marital bedroom. Offscreen sound is particularly ominous. Octavio, brooding in his blue bedroom, cannot bear to hear his brother Ramiro making love with Susana through the paper-thin wall. Heightening our identification with him, the spectator also hears but does not see the noisy sex. Octavio interrupts the married couple, claiming that Susana has a phone call. When she finds no one is there, Octavio admits the silent call was from him. Contrary to first impressions once more, *Amores Perros* is hardly a 'two-hour shout'. Frequently the film falls silent. Perhaps the most memorable moments are those when words fail: Octavio looks out in despair from the window after Susana has fled, as does Valeria when the apartment has become her prison; El Chivo gazes across the street at the daughter to whom he cannot speak. These eloquent but silent images were so characteristic of the film that they graced the US poster.

Speech in the first episode is either elaborately profane and idiosyncratically slangy (e.g. the Mexican 'chido' for 'cool') or achingly simple. Octavio and Susana's doomed affair can be charted in the subtly modulated words they repeat in the bedroom and funeral parlour: 'You don't get it'; 'Now I get it'; 'You still don't get it'. Crucially, however, all the dialogue is diegetic, sourced within the story space and time. In spite of the complexity of its overlapping triple narratives, *Amores Perros* refuses the easy way out of a voice-over that would either direct the audience from outside the fiction (telling us why, for example, Susana abandoned Octavio) or would grant the characters themselves retrospective knowledge (showing us how, for example, Octavio learned from his experience). All three episodes remain, finally, open, both in their stories and their sound design.

González Iñárritu fully exploits the resources of diegetic sound, especially sudden changes in volume. In the first episode Octavio's voluble and volatile household is crosscut with that of the solitary El Chivo. The latter is given much complex action to carry off (a murder, the discovery in the newspaper of his wife's death) without a word of dialogue. Valeria's tumultuous car crash gives way to the hushed hospital and isolated apartment. Only Richi's yapping plays over a black screen as his mistress returns home. In this second episode, offscreen sound is thematised once more. The attempt to locate Richi beneath the floor tiles is at once narrative and acoustic, as the poodle's whimpering and scampering migrate worryingly over the multi-channel sound. Up in the middle of the night, hushed to hear the lost poodle, Daniel and Valeria are shocked by the ringing of the phone (disparity in volume once more). It is a sound used (we assume) by Daniel's wife to torture her rival, just as she had been tortured by it before. Naturalistic, diegetic sound is thus written into the plot, with the wounded lovers (and attentive audience) acoustically sensitive as never before.

Gustavo Santaolalla's theme, suddenly prominent an hour into the film, makes some delicate connections here. As a dreamy soundbridge, it links Daniel tending to the crippled Valeria with El Chivo nursing the wounded Cofi. With the addition of an ominously wailing synthesiser, it accompanies Daniel first with Valeria and then without as they gaze (he gazes) out at the mocking poster on painful nights. But González Iñárritu also allows himself subjective sound here. Shots of that symbolic space below the floor (in the house but alien to it) are shown over a rumbling, volcanic sound that goes unexplained. Clearly this sound is emblematic of the black hole, at once physical and metaphorical, into which the briefly happy couple have fallen. With Valeria back in hospital for the second time, Daniel is alone in the empty flat whose silence, shockingly once more, will be shattered by a frenzied assault on the tiles that finally retrieves Richi. But in this chamber piece of an episode González Iñárritu retains his reticence still. No music accompanies the most dramatic moment: Daniel's discovery of Valeria unconscious on the floor. In spite, then, of the superficial similarity of such scenes to Mexican popular melodrama, *Amores Perros* is never further from the telenovelas than in its sound design: the latter ceaselessly signal each changing mood (humorous, amorous, tragic) with cheesy musical prompts.

Yet more subtly González Iñárritu uses acoustic connections to forge chains of meaning through the film. One daring soundbridge, jumping across time and space, is the ringing phone that sounds over the fade of the second episode (Daniel and Valeria embracing as they face the void) but is sourced in the opening shot of the third episode. There we learn

The space below the floor

that it comes from the mobile belonging to businessman Gustavo, which will soon be thrown from the window of the speeding car by bent cop Leonardo. The telltale sound of the phone heralds yet another betrayal: Gustavo will trick his half-brother just as Daniel dumped his wife and, before that, Octavio seduced his sister-in-law. Found music is also increasingly prominent as the film develops. The second montage sequence plays over 1980s rock anthem 'Lucha de gigantes'/'Battle of the Giants'. Where the Mexican Control Machete seemed appropriate to the hard-edged urban imagery of the first montage, Nacha Pop's Spanish romanticism heightens a dissonance already evident on the image track: the young lovers' urgent lovemaking is crosscut with Ramiro's abduction and brutal beating by the thugs paid by Octavio. The impressionistic lyricism of 'Lucha de gigantes', so different to Control Machete's visceral minimalism, gestures towards narrative themes that cannot be made explicit in the sparse dialogue: the singer, pursed by a nameless beast, feels he and his lover are so fragile in a world that is just too big. This is perhaps the only (oblique) reference in the film to the unsustainable size of Mexico D.F. The song lends the inarticulate underclass a voice with which to abstract and universalise their nightmarish predicament in the extreme city.

The original soundtrack is surprisingly diverse with Gustavo Santaolalla employing such urban found materials as PVC pipes, custard moulds and tin-can violins. The second-hand songs are also very varied. Executive producer Martha Sosa told me that the choice of Nacha Pop, now incongruously outdated, was a 'sentimental caprice' on González Iñárritu's part. They had both been involved with the Spanish act when they were music promoters and still loved the song. Certainly the fact that 'Lucha de gigantes' is repeated over the closing credits gives it a lingering authority. Less romantically, *Screen International* reported on 9 June 2000 that production company Altavista aimed to put together a slate of 'teen targeted films with compelling soundtracks', exploiting holding company CIE's links with the music industry. Local bands, typical of contemporary D.F., are juxtaposed with Spanish rockers Nacha Pop, Cuban salsa veteran Celia Cruz and British popsters the Hollies, whose 'Long Cool

Woman in a Black Dress' plays idiosyncratically over the most Tarantino-esque scene in the film, El Chivo's torture of his kidnapped victims. Crucially, however, very little of this music is clearly audible in the final cut of the film. The lyrics of both Cruz's very general plea for optimism in the face of adversity ('La vida es un carnaval'/'Life Is a Carnival') and Banda Espuela de Oro's very specific attack on the corruption of the Mexican government ('Dame el poder'/'Give Me the Power') are near undetectable in the mix. The musical, as well as the political, message of *Amores Perros* remains emotionally potent but unspecified. Lynn Fainchtein, the musical supervisor of the film (as of all Altavista releases), not only has work experience with MTV, but also possesses a degree in psychology from the national university, UNAM.

The musical diversity of *Amores Perros*'s soundtrack, at once pleasurable and problematic, reflects what Michel Chion has called the 'false Esperanto' of movie music:

Cinema is the art par excellence in which all kinds of music have right of residence [*droit de cité*] and where, sometimes within the same work, styles and periods are juxtaposed and collapsed together … Film fans who go to the cinema and hear jazz may believe they understand it, when in fact they only capture the surface: the quality of the sound, of the voice, of the phrasing escape them. The same may well be true of other aspects of the film, such as the texture of its dialogue or its observational qualities in relation to its subject – but the problem with music is the illusion that one has an immediate communication with it.[33]

Responding immediately to the very attractive rhythms of *Amores Perros*'s soundtrack, global audiences may also fool themselves that they have an intimate communion with the songs, while they can hardly convince themselves they understand the dialogue unless they have a working knowledge of Mexican Spanish. The 'false common language' of sound[34] masks distinctions between D.F. and the Caribbean, the Americas and Europe, which are accessible only to those familiar with the many popular musics of a huge and diverse Spanish-speaking world.

There is no doubt that outside the immediate context of the feature film the soundtrack was conceived as an independent entity. The musicians featured on the soundtrack were involved in the production process. After being shown an early cut of *Amores Perros* they wrote songs inspired by the film that were released to coincide with the film's Mexican premiere. I mentioned earlier that a concert of local stars formed part of the promotional package. González Iñárritu also used his skills as a DJ to craft the CD soundtrack into a pseudo-cinematic narrative. The disc begins with the uncanny whooshing noise that evokes speeding cars, subterranean tremors and panting dogs. The songs that follow are crosscut with Santaolalla's haunting theme, which develops throughout the disc, climaxing with the uncanny pizzicato or glissando effect (the tin-can violins?) which accompanies El Chivo's journey into the wilderness. The names given to the various versions of the theme on the CD make explicit the relation between sound and space ('The Apartment'), sound and time ('Memories'), and sound and narrative ('Finding Love'). Some songs are distorted as if heard through the car radio, others (like the golden oldie 'Long Cool Woman') are introduced by tacky station jingles.

The second CD, music inspired by the film, is equally diverse. As if attempting to undercut the stereotype of urban grunge (just as González Iñárritu had tried to stop *Amores Perros* being branded as a 'dogfighting movie'), many of the featured songs are surprisingly delicate. Control Machete's 'Amores perros: de perros amores', which was used for the theatrical trailer but not in the film itself, is a case in point. It begins as a hard chanted rap treating social problems ('The problems of just one day are enough/to worry you for the whole future') but is soon interrupted by an ethereal female vocal which is decidedly more abstract ('Dawn breaks in the soul/the sun sets in you'). The effect is somewhat similar to Eminem's sampling of Dido. Two songs whose promos are featured as extras on the DVD also suggest a more sensitive, even reflective, mood that belies visceral hollering. Julieta Venegas's melancholic 'Amores perros me van a matar'/'*Amores perros* Will Be the Death of Me' and Café Tacuba's delicately masochistic 'Amores perros: aviéntame'/'*Amores perros*: Cut Me Up' both gently lament lost love that has given no happiness and has left the lover's body undone. The physical force of the film is here subtly transformed into musical melancholy. If we listen more closely, then, the acoustic patterning of *Amores Perros* and its rich variations in texture are so strong as to transcend the film itself. As *Le Monde* suggested of González Iñárritu's surprising and troubling 'art', sound design takes the film and the listener out of themselves to new and unexpected places.

6 Slaves to the Image

Vaya pesadilla, corriendo
Con una bestia detrás.
Dime que es mentira, todo
Un sueño tonto, y no más.
Me da miedo la enormidad
Donde nadie oye mi voz.

What a nightmare, running
With a wild beast on my heels.
Tell me it's all a lie,
Just a stupid dream.
I'm afraid of the immensity
Where no one can hear my voice.

Nacha Pop, 'Lucha de gigantes'

Michel Chion, who stresses the relative autonomy of the Dolby soundtrack, also insists that sound cannot be wholly independent of image. His position is extreme:

There is no soundtrack. ... A film's aural elements are not received as an autonomous unit. They are immediately analysed and distributed in the spectator's perceptual apparatus according to what the spectator sees at the time [in an] instantaneous perceptual triage.[35]

It remains the case, however, that just as *Amores Perros*'s sound design deserves to be taken on its own merits, so its visuals require separate consideration. Although, as Chion writes once more, 'if you alter or remove the sounds, the image is no longer the same',[36] it is revealing to watch the film on mute without subtitles. Only then do we realise how much of the complex narrative structure is carried by the image track.

A good example comes 32 minutes in. González Iñárritu cuts directly from the whirling inferno of the dogfight to a peaceful exterior. It is a long shot of black-clothed mourners against a blurry white background of tombstones. A reverse angle shows El Chivo in medium shot framed by green foliage, his tangled mane haloed by back lighting. Inching closer, the camera shows his weeping daughter Maru turn to embrace her tense, skinny aunt. The latter looks up and her eyes harden in horror when they meet El Chivo's. After walking slowly up to him, the aunt (played by the excellent Rosa María Bianchi) engages him warily in a brief conversation before turning on her heels and stalking away. The conflict between the characters is clearly shown in the physical expressions of the actors. But it is also manifest in the contrasts in background: El Chivo is shot against the tree; the aunt in front of the tombs. When we turn up the sound the dialogue ('What are you doing here?'; 'Just taking a stroll') adds little to the intense emotional effect of this short scene, just one and a half minutes long.

Vision (like sound) is thematised in the film, turned into part of the plot. Daniel and Valeria are slaves to the image, dependent on mechanical reproduction for their livelihood, even their lives. El Chivo's psychic or ethical arc is imaged in his physical or visual transformation. We see him cutting matted hair, beard and toenails and exchanging grungy garments for relatively salubrious blazer and trousers. The trace of his travails remains, however, in the battered shoes and broken glasses, mended with tape. If the problem of the script was to preserve continuity of perspective among a large ensemble cast, then point of view is also highlighted in the physical action. El Chivo, who has hitherto refused to see clearly (claiming God had wished his sight to be blurry), puts on his glasses for the first time after Cofi has killed his canine family. This is the most explicit point-of-view shot in the film: El Chivo's decrepit ceiling suddenly comes into sharp focus, with the photo of his beloved daughter shown upside down from the father's perspective. Typically, once more, González Iñárritu uses no language here. This pivotal point, in which El Chivo gives up his career in killing and returns to human intercourse, is shown in strictly visual terms.

Throughout *Amores Perros* the resources of *mise en scène* (that is, the visual elements within the frame) are used to differentiate people and places from one another. Octavio's soiled international sportswear (including a T-shirt, borrowed from Jorge, with Wes Craven's 'Scream' logo) is implicitly contrasted with Daniel's starched shirts (who launders them now he has left the family home?). The third episode implies a synthesis to this antithesis, when the transformed El Chivo takes on some of the class distinction of sharp-suited businessmen Luis and Gustavo (along with their car and mobile phone). Costume seems, like music, to be a more accessible means of distinction than language. Few listeners will catch the change in register between El Chivo's slangy and distinctively Mexican greeting '¿Quiúbole, bróder?' ('Whassup, bro'?') and Gustavo's respectful response 'Mucho gusto' ('Pleased to meet you'). No spectator can miss the difference in their clothes.

Costume also interacts with set design. Although all of the locations are 'authentic' and thus supposedly natural, they are artfully dressed to carry

El Chivo's glasses

El Chivo's perspective

social and psychological connotations. The house Octavio shares with his mother, brother and sister-in-law is dense with objects that crowd the frame. And as an indiscriminate teenager, his walls, TV and even wallet are covered with colourful stickers. In contrast Daniel and Valeria's dream apartment is airy and neutral, coloured, like their costumes, cool blue and pale green. The only splash of blood red is the mocking Enchant poster glimpsed from the window. Maru's house has splashes of bright pink and yellow, evoking Mexican modernists like Luis Barragán who, unlike their fellow International Stylists, mixed strong colours with geometric form. Her family's cultural status is signalled by a Matisse-like collage on the wall, also vividly coloured. On the other hand fat Mauricio's kitsch statue of Venus (with electric lights flashing up and down its exterior) signals a proletarian taste. Briefly but reverently caught in close-up, it is characteristic of *Amores Perros*'s art design, which transcends documentary realism without stridently calling attention to itself. Aesthetic pleasure is found in the most unlikely places. Skin, authentically fleshy at home, is tinged an unearthly green under fluorescent lights that chromatically link locations that are distant in time, space and class: Ramiro's supermarket, Valeria's hospital and the funeral home where Octavio and Susana speak for the last time.

This strategy of graphic contrast or visual clashing emerged in pre-production. The scrapbook at Altavista's office features collages of found images clipped from magazines: a reclining model is juxtaposed with a hospital doctor and a group of dogs tied to a car. Or again, evoking the working title of the film ('Perro negro/Perro blanco'), a snarling black dog is set against a bikini-clad blonde promenading her white poodle at the beach. Combining the local and the global once more, street shots of Mexican youths posing obligingly for the location scout are glued on the same page as Nan Goldin's artfully composed studies of tearful domestic squalor in New York, Paris and Bangkok.

Goldin has often been cited as a visual source for the art design of *Amores Perros*. It is clear that there are many formal and even iconographic similarities between the two: the saturated colour, grainy texture and tight composition; the exploitation of mirrors and claustrophobically darkened exteriors. Less obvious, but perhaps equally important, is Goldin's potent use of the visual to tell stories even without words. In exhibition (for example, at London's Whitechapel Gallery in spring 2002), her photographs are 'framed' by room titles ('Lovers', 'Loss', 'Recovery') as abstract and poignant as *Amores Perros*'s 'Love is . . .' tag lines; they are grouped together in chronological or thematic grids (charting Cookie or Gilles's harrowing loss to AIDS); or, more cinematically still, they are strung into lengthy slide shows that are set to apparently incongruous music (liturgical songs from Björk over graphic sex scenes). The differences, however, are equally obvious. Although both Goldin and González Iñárritu are resolutely urban artists, *Amores Perros* shows no interest in Goldin's subcultures of drag queens and junkies. Nor does the film take pleasure in places of entertainment (apart from the dogfights of course). To cite Goldin's favourite Velvet Underground titles, *Amores Perros* tells Mexicans 'I'll Be Your Mirror', but does not mournfully commemorate 'All Tomorrow's Parties'. Festivity is conspicuously absent from the film's version of the metropolis.

Goldin's work is far more diverse and technically skilled than is commonly thought, with recent work chronicling childbirth and old age with classical rigour. But *Amores Perros*'s 'look' is equally varied and complex. In a fascinating interview with *American Cinematographer*, director of photography Rodrigo Prieto revealed how it was done. Prieto, who had already won Ariels for previous Mexican features, explained that he wanted 'a very specific grain structure', which was achieved by the risky technique of 'a bleach-bypass process on the camera negative':

The contrast in general is enhanced with skip-bleach, but so is the contrast of the grain ... [The process] desaturates certain hues and colours, such as skin tones, but the reds and blues [are] even enhance[d] ... We wanted the film to feel realistic, but with an edge. We were after the power of imperfection [and wanted to] use 'mistakes' to enhance the urgency and unpredictability of life in a place like Mexico City.[37]

Most difficult of all was the apparently naturalistic scene of the car chase. Prieto continues:

The skip bleach is so extreme that if I had shot the scene with natural light, the exteriors would have been white, with practically no detail outside the vehicle ... Most of the time I was tied onto [Octavio's] hood, handholding the camera, with lights and diffusion attached all around me. The challenge was to make it look as if it wasn't lit![38]

'Natural light' thus proves to be the most artificial of all. The finely crafted cinematography served both to bring together and to draw apart the three episodes. All the footage was treated with skip-bleach, but the second episode was shot on a different film to make it 'crisper and cleaner'. Real fluorescents were used to light night scenes, producing the greenish hue noted earlier. Different lenses were used for each episode: a wider lens for 'Octavio' where the camera kept close to the actors; a long lens, including a zoom, for 'El Chivo' 'to further isolate the man from his environment'. The shooting style also varied, with the camera handling in the first episode being 'rhythmic' and 'aggressive', the second 'more static', and the third (Prieto's favourite) 'both edgy and elegant'.[39]

Camera height, distance and movement are important too. In the first episode Prieto gets down and dirty with the dogs, shooting the snarling battles at floor height. Interestingly, however, this position recurs in the second episode, where camera height decreases as the horror increases. By

Daniel breaks down the door

the end Daniel is shot breaking down the door from floor height, ready for the discovery of the collapsed Valeria in the next shot. The very last shot of the film, the black landscape into which El Chivo and Cofi disappear, is shown from the same low angle. This contrasts with the penultimate shot: a horizontal pan of the desolate scene from El Chivo's point of view.

Camera distance varies as much as camera height. Octavio and Susana's exchanges are shown in close-ups that edge ever tighter as the young couple become more intimate with each other and the audience. But the same technique is used for lovers Daniel and Valeria when they first return from hospital. Extreme close-ups suggest a new intimacy between this superficial couple and direct new sympathy towards them from the spectator. González Iñárritu tends to begin sequences with an extreme close-up rather than the wide shot that conventionally serves to establish a new location. For example, on the three occasions that a scene starts with a TV screen filling the frame, we subsequently find out that we are first in Octavio's bedroom, then in Daniel's and finally in the studio itself: the camera pulls back to reveal we are watching a monitor on the set of the chat show where Valeria and Andrés have been feigning love. At other points the camera keeps its distance. Ramiro's first robbery, which could have been a chance for graphic, violent action, is filmed in long shot from outside the pharmacy window, thus distancing us. Later we will be taken inside the bank for Ramiro's climactic and deadly shoot-out. When Octavio and Susana have their last, wrenching encounter we see them not in the usual tight close-up but in a sustained two-shot which heightens the tension and distance between them.

But if González Iñárritu often fails to begin sequences with the classic wide shot, he generally shoots conversation in traditional style as shot/counter shot, albeit with an edgily mobile hand-held camera that is constantly reframing the actors. Sometimes, however, the camera swings dizzily from one speaker to another, as in the scene on the roof where Cofi fights for the first time in Mauricio's house. While this feels appropriate for a dramatically tense sequence (but note how the fight itself is offscreen and registers only as sound), elsewhere conspicuous camera movement is avoided. One shot in which Prieto circled around the immobilised Valeria, which reportedly made the cinematographer quite sick, was omitted from the final cut but is included among the deleted sequences on the DVD. There is, to my knowledge, not one crane shot in *Amores Perros* even when circumstances seem to cry out for it, as when El Chivo disappears into the desert.

Just as the film falls silent at significant moments, so the camera simply comes to a halt at certain points, as if mesmerised by subtle performance. The complicated exposition of El Chivo's back story (he is a Marxist guerrilla turned hit man) is narrated by Leonardo the cop to Gustavo the businessman in a fast-moving car with a constantly changing background. In contrast El Chivo's telephone confession to his daughter is filmed in a single static shot for some two and a half minutes without a break. The only other take in the film to last so long has a very different effect. A vertiginous steadycam follows Octavio out to his car with the wounded Cofi, back to the dogfighting den where he stabs El Jarocho, and then, in a visceral rush, back again to the car where the camera rests for a full three seconds on a textured tableau: the bloody red blade abandoned on a cracked grey pavement. The psychological length of a take is inseparable from camera movement and plot exposition. The first scene seems to go on for ever as the old man tearfully confesses his true story; the second seems over in a flash as the young man rushes towards the fateful and futile car crash.

The TV monitor on the set

Octavio and Susana in two shot

Leonardo and Gustavo in the car

El Chivo's telephone confession

González Iñárritu is a veteran of pop promos and advertising spots, both genres which privilege graphic immediacy. But the cinematic techniques used in *Amores Perros* also echo the highly literate script, by novelist Guillermo Arriaga. Arriaga's fiction *Un dulce olor a muerte/Sweet Smell of Death* (1994) prefigures aspects of *Amores Perros*. It begins with a penetrating scream 'offscreen', as it were; offers visceral 'close-ups' (a cockroach crushed beneath a bare foot); and 'cuts' from one point of view to another as it explores a single, fatal incident. The graphic, but never flashy, editing style in *Amores Perros* is also justified by the screenplay, which interweaves the different narratives, locations and social classes. Moreover there is no consistent 'MTV style', which González Iñárritu's commercial background might encourage him to adopt. He does not lean too heavily on music. And if *Amores Perros*'s action sequences often benefit from mobile camerawork and quick cutting, this is not always the case. One of the pop videos directed by González Iñárritu and included as an extra on the DVD (the delicate acoustic ballad 'Amores perros: aviéntame' by Café Tacuba) is edited so it appears to be a single shot. The camera whip pans from one mismatched couple to another (elderly man and young woman, young mother and suicidal lover), all photographed in the grainy, saturated style recognisable from the feature.

González Iñárritu's musical background leaves him, nonetheless, highly sensitive to the rhythmic value of editing. The masterful theatrical trailer features not one word of dialogue, but simply cuts from one intensely emotional moment to another at an increasingly breakneck velocity. At the climax subliminal frames of violent action, visible only on the DVD, punctuate the last seconds of close-up montage. The new medium of DVD also implies new forms of the consumption of images, to which *Amores Perros* is sensitive. The disc contains an unusually large number of options for a Spanish-language feature. The original artfully off-centre framing can now be savoured or even modified by the zoom button. The perfect freeze frame also allows us to eavesdrop, as it were, on each image in turn, uncovering elements hidden to theatre audiences. For example, we can actually read the letter Valeria takes momentarily from her box of mementos, sent to her by an affectionate young relative.

(The letter appears to be sent to the actress herself, addressed as it is to 'Yoyes', a diminutive form of 'Goya'.) The highly crafted *mise en scène* is rendered yet more visible.

The deleted sequences, complete with director's commentary, and the 'campaign development' section, showing successive versions of the poster in the UK and US, seem at first to demystify the production process, taking away the power and immediacy with which unsuspecting spectators faced the film in cinemas. In practice, however, such extras reveal that just as the ambitious sound design of *Amores Perros* cannot be confined to the feature itself, so its consistent look expands to embrace other cultural objects. The final posters with their distinctive colour scheme (black, white and red) and tripartite division (three faces of one film) are all of a piece with the film's graphic style and narrative structure. The UK DVD menu screen, red swatches of colour over a degraded black cityscape, evokes extreme urbanism as strongly as any image in the film itself. The distinctive Cannes press kit came in an elongated, letter-box format and boasted gorgeously distorted images of the actors, both human and animal, merging and disintegrating into blurred go-faster stripes.

From page to screen González Iñárritu did not cease to increase the visual charge of *Amores Perros*. The last version of Arriaga's script contains at least two scenes that have been heightened in the shoot. In the first,

Gael García's 'unforgettable eyes'

Octavio plays with a knife as he discusses entering Cofi in the contest: in the film he tenderly bathes his dog. In the second, El Chivo shoots his first victim on the way to his car, and not, as in the film, in the more incongruous and spectacular setting of a Japanese restaurant.

If we look and listen closely enough to *Amores Perros*, then, we discover that the naively expressive model of creativity is not appropriate here. Although González Iñárritu may call the film a 'visceral shout' or 'scream', the undeniable, even overwhelming, emotions it produces in the audience derive not from one individual psyche but from a multitude of expert collaborators. Even praise of an actor as gifted and charismatic as Gael García gains from some technical knowledge of the film's production process. Would Gael's eyes have been as 'unforgettable' as critics remarked had their whites not been highlighted by the skip-bleach process? Certainly in his next starring role, Alfonso Cuarón's sexy and funny road movie *Y tu mamá también/And Your Mother Too* (2001), he no longer seems enhanced by the heroic, even tragic, stature that González Iñárritu coaxed out of his diminutive frame. What González Iñárritu and his faithful team knew instinctively is that true art hides its own artifice. But it is this dangerous and elusive artistic supplement, noted by *Le Monde*, that distances *Amores Perros* from documentary realism even as it engages the audience most deeply with the intense and tender human experience depicted in the film.

Epilogue: Mexico Cinema, 2002

The script posits a synthesis: the life of a man divided into three characters –
a boy under twenty, a man of forty, and a man of sixty ... The three discover
who they are and become themselves. They discover that pain is also a path
toward hope. It is in these conclusions that the characters converge.[40]

Screen International (which had published the 'case study' of *Amores
Perros*'s production history) recently ran a 'territory focus' on Mexico.
Under the headline 'New Mexico' and beneath a picture of Gael García's
Octavio, eyes blazing silver with skip-bleach, Anna Marie de la Fuente
began by claiming that *Amores Perros*'s Oscar nomination and
'unprecedented international success' was just 'the crest of a wave'. The
film is the culmination of a wider trend in Mexico: 'Over recent years the
territory has established itself both as a source of edgy, contemporary films
and as a major market for distributors. Right now, Mexico is the darling of
Latin America.'[41]

Exhibition, production and distribution are equally strong.
Increasing numbers of young cinemagoers and multiplex growth have
given Mexico almost 3,000 screens, the biggest number in Latin America
(double that of Brazil, a country twice as populous as Mexico). Thanks to
hits such as *Amores Perros* and *Y tu mamá también*, 'local productions have
increased their market share from 3% in 1995 to nearly 20% in 2001'.
Distributors have also spent 'unprecedented sums on p&a [prints and
advertising]' (de la Fuente cites *Amores Perros* and *Vivir mata* as evidence
here). Artistic trends have also changed. Neglecting the now
'conventional' magical realism of, say, Alfonso Arau's *Like Water for
Chocolate*, new producers favour 'gritty social commentaries'.

What is the secret of this success? New president Vicente Fox had
announced in autumn 2001 that production should be expanded to an
ambitious sixty films a year by 2006. An amended film law has injected
$7.4 million of government funding. More important perhaps is that, after
changes in tax law in late 1999, 'financing from private film companies has
exceeded that of the national film institute, IMCINE'. *Y tu mamá también*,

incongruously perhaps, was wholly financed by a nutritional supplements corporation. *Amores Perros*'s Altavista and Tequila Gang (Guillermo del Toro's *El espinazo del Diablo/The Devil's Backbone*) are named as established producers. The new production house of teen comedy *Inspiración* was the first to secure distribution from a US studio: Fox. Foreign distributors have picked up other films for the global market, including Rafael Montero's *Corazones rotos*. Meanwhile Mexico, and especially the capital, continues to attract foreign productions, with 'world class studios', such as Fox Baja, which had hosted *Titanic*.

This report was only the latest of a number of optimistic articles in the trade press. Not for the first time they clashed with the pessimistic opinions of academic commentators. Charles Ramírez Berg,[42] Néstor García Canclini[43] and John King[44] coincide in proclaiming the desperate straits of Mexican cinema. In this they agree with the national film school[45] and journalist and author Jorge Ayala Blanco,[46] who has been predicting the death of Mexican cinema for some twenty years.

While Ayala's diagnosis of the 'precariousness' ('fugacidad') of recent production is surely correct, much of the difference between trade and academic perspectives comes from their respective biases: business will tend to favour private investment, leftist scholars public protectionism. In spite of a recent decline in the number of films made (offset by their greater popularity with youthful Mexican audiences), it seems likely that Mexican cinema has, for the moment at least, achieved that holy grail of film-making in a medium-sized country: reconciling art and commerce. It has done this by avoiding, on the one hand, paternalist corruption and, on the other, capitalist degradation. It is a model that might be imitated by countries such as the UK. If foreign filmgoers are to appreciate such films, however (and Britons were almost deprived of the chance to see *Amores Perros*), they will need energetic and skilful distributors such as Optimum Releasing. When *Amores Perros* won a British Academy award, the latter proudly announced in a press release that they specialised in 'dynamic, intelligent, market-driven product'.[47]

The possibility of a Mexican director sustaining a long-term career (the problem identified by González Iñárritu himself) remains open. The

record of earlier directors has been chequered. Jaime Humberto
Hermosillo, who remains perhaps the only openly gay director in Latin
America, has long been reduced to microbudgets. Arturo Ripstein, who
uniquely perhaps has worked consistently for some three decades, has seen
himself sidelined by new trends. Nicolás Echevarría released his second
feature *Vivir mata* over a decade after his first, *Cabeza de Vaca*. González
Iñárritu had been vociferous in attacking earlier film-makers, telling *Sight
and Sound* that he and Guillermo Arriaga 'loathe the government-financed
movie-making that seems to operate by the maxim: "If nobody understands
and nobody goes to see a movie, that must mean it's a masterpiece."'[48] It is
populist talk directed against art directors such as Ripstein, who was quoted
as saying at Cannes (where his own film was overshadowed by *Amores
Perros*): 'I don't make films for idiots' (*El Universal*, 19 May 2000).

González Iñárritu himself has expressed an affinity for Mexican
directors who have worked in Hollywood, telling *Hispanic* magazine (April
2001) that he feels no responsibility to represent Latino audiences and
refuses to be limited to an ethnic niche. And *Screen International*
announced on 19 July 2002 that his long awaited follow-up (working title:
21 Grams) would be shot in English and star Benicio del Toro and Sean
Penn. *Amores Perros*'s final credits name Alfonso Cuarón and Guillermo
del Toro (both of whom have made English-language pictures in the US)
among a long list of 'impossible without … '. *Amores Perros* is already a
hybrid, combining Hollywood-friendly form with preoccupations typical of
mexicanidad, albeit disguised by seductive sound and vision.

It is a synthesis typical of what screenwriter Arriaga dares to call
Amores Perros's 'dialectic':

First to have a thesis with a very realistic and dramatic story, to go to an
antithesis that is absurd, in very closed spaces with very few characters, and
a synthesis, where we have a psychological thriller where the other two
stories get mixed.[49]

The characters are also mixed, both good and bad. Octavio and Daniel are
at once adulterous and faithful to their new loves. El Chivo is an idealist

who becomes a terrorist and is then redeemed. Simple Susana is ultimately loyal to the husband who beat her and vain Valeria is purged by bitter sacrifice. The pessimistic ending of the script (shots ring out in El Chivo's house where the two brothers are confined) gives way to the open ending of the film (the old man sets out towards the future with that other tamed killer, Cofi). There is a hidden personal reference here also: Cofi is renamed 'Negro', the nickname of the director himself.

'Dialectic' is perhaps the answer also to the vexed question of *Amores Perros*'s politics. In his moving account of poverty and distress in French society, *The Weight of the World*, Pierre Bourdieu had, like Arriaga, cited modernist precedents such as Faulkner for his technique: a 'juxtaposition' revealing the 'tragic consequences of incompatible points of view'.[50] Abandoning the 'single, central, dominant' viewpoint for a 'multiplicity of coexisting and competing' perspectives, both works reveal 'the complexity and ambiguity of human experience … bringing together individuals who otherwise have nothing in common'.[51] The only problem is that Arriaga delights in the fact that 'life is relative' and *Amores Perros* offers no 'lesson in morality': 'Ethical judgments had to come from the spectator, not from the film.'[52] However, he also laments the absence of a 'guiding authority to bring dialogue and consensus', which has led to the loss of fraternity and 'intolerable levels of violence'.[53] Hence the absence of fathers in the film and the theme of fratricidal rivalry.

But Arriaga qualifies his position. *Amores Perros* is ethical after all: 'implicit in every aesthetic is an ethic'.[54] And the sheer ambition of González Iñárritu's film is perhaps its most outstanding characteristic, daring as it does to present a grand mosaic of the metropolis worthy of the nineteenth-century novel. *Amores Perros* could not be further, then, from a postmodern irony that is now exhausted. Fiercely emotional, but never sentimental, ethically serious, but never pious, it is a uniquely powerful work in world cinema.

Notes

1 Guillermo Arriaga, 'Perro negro/perro blanco' [unpublished shooting script, with corrections by hand], dated 30 March 1999.

2 Anna Marie de la Fuente, 'Case Study: Amores Perros', Screen International no. 1315, 6–12 July 2001, p. 17.

3 Ibid.

4 The following account of domestic promotion is based on private documents held in Altavista's Mexico City office.

5 Carlos Pedroza and Alfonso Flores-Durán, 'Amores perros: a la pelea con los críticos de Cannes', Cine XS, June 2000, pp. 34–5 (p. 34).

6 Jorge Ayala Blanco, La fugacidad del cine mexicano (Mexico City: Océano, 2001), p. 485.

7 Ibid., p. 486.

8 Leonardo García Tsao, 'Elogios a Amores Perros' [Cannes location report], La Jornada, 15 May 2000, unnumbered press clipping.

9 Néstor García Canclini (ed.), Los nuevos espectadores: cine, televisión, y video en México (Mexico City: IMCINE/CONACULTA, 1994), p. 14.

10 Ibid., p. 294.

11 Ibid., p. 216.

12 Ibid., p. 334.

13 Ibid., p. 342.

14 Patricia Torres San Martín, 'Los perros amores de los tapatíos' [research paper on audiences in Guadalajara], unpublished.

15 José Arroyo, review of Amores Perros, Sight and Sound, May 2001, pp. 39–40.

16 Charles Ramírez Berg, Cinema of Solitude: A Critical Study of Mexican Film, 1967–1983 (Austin: University of Texas, 1992), p. 2.

17 Ibid., p. 3.

18 Ibid., pp. 22–7.

19 Ibid., p. 28.

20 Álvaro Cueva, Sangre de mi sangre: verdades y mentiras de las telenovelas en América Latina (Mexico City: Plaza y Janés, 2001), passim.

21 Ibid., p. 142.

22 Berg, Cinema of Solitude, p. 56.

23 Ibid., p. 55.

24 Carlos Monsiváis, 'Mythologies', in Paulo Antonio Paranaguá (ed.), Mexican Cinema (London: BFI, 1995), pp. 117–27 (p. 119).

25 Cueva, Sangre de mi sangre, p. 143.

26 Altavista, Amores perros/Amours chiennes/Love's a Bitch [Cannes pressbook] (2000), unpaginated.

27 Françoise Audé, 'Désirs aveugles, fantômes futurs' [review and interview with Alejandro González Iñárritu], Positif no. 477, November 2000, pp. 22–8 (p. 22).

28 Ibid., p. 28.

29 David Stratton, review of Amores Perros, Variety, 22–8 May 2000, p. 24.

30 'L'Amour, chien de l'enfer des villes' [review of Amores Perros], Le Monde, 1 November 2000, p. 29.

31 Jonathan Romney, 'Going to the Dogs' [interview with Alejandro González Iñárritu], Guardian, 22 August 2000, section 2, pp. 12–13.

32 Michel Chion, The Voice in Cinema (New York: Columbia University Press, 1999), p. 166.

33 Michel Chion, La Musique au cinéma (Paris: Fayard, 1995), p. 17.

34 Ibid., p. 18.

35 Chion, The Voice in Cinema, pp. 1, 3.

36 Ibid., p. 4.

37 Jean Oppenheimer, 'A Dog's Life' [interview with Rodrigo Prieto], American Cinematographer vol. 82 no. 4, April 2001, pp. 20–9 (pp. 20, 23).

38 Ibid., p. 28.

39 Ibid., p. 24.

40 Guillermo Arriaga, *Amores Perros* [script], trans. Alan Page (London: Faber, 2001), p. x.

41 Anna Marie de la Fuente, 'Territory Focus: Mexico', *Screen International* no. 1345, 22–8 February 2002, pp. 12–13.

42 Berg, *Cinema of Solitude*, passim.

43 García Canclini, *Los nuevos espectadores*, passim.

44 John King, *Magical Reels*, second edn. (London: Verso, 2000).

45 Centro de Capacitación Cinematográfica, *1975–2000* (Mexico: CONACULTA, 2001).

46 Ayala Blanco, *La fugacidad*, passim.

47 Optimum Releasing, '*Amores Perros* Wins BAFTA' [press release] (London), 26 February 2002.

48 Bernardo Pérez Soler, 'Pup Fiction' [interview with Alejandro González Iñárritu], *Sight and Sound*, May 2001, pp. 29–30 (p. 29).

49 Peter N. Chumo II, 'Script Review: *Amores Perros*', *Creative Screenwriting* vol. 8 no. 2, March–April 2001, pp. 10–12 (p. 12).

50 Pierre Bourdieu, *The Weight of the World* (Cambridge: Polity, 1999), p. 3.

51 Ibid., p. 4.

52 Arriaga, *Amores Perros* [script], pp. ix, x.

53 Ibid., pp. viii, ix.

54 Ibid., pp. x.

Credits

AMORES PERROS
(Love's a Bitch)

Mexico 2000

Director
Alejandro González Iñárritu
Producer
Alejandro González Iñárritu
Screenplay
Guillermo Arriaga Jordán
Director of Photography
Rodrigo Prieto
Editors
Alejandro González Iñárritu
Luis Carballar
Fernando Pérez Unda
Production Designer
Brigitte Broch
Music
Gustavo Santaolalla
© Altavista Films, S.A,
Z Film.

Production Companies
Altavista Films presents a
Zeta Film and Altavista
Films production
Executive Producers
Martha Sosa Elizondo
Francisco González
Compeán
Associate Producers
Raúl Olvera Ferrer
Guillermo Arriaga Jordán
Pelayo Gutiérrez
Monica Lozano Serrano
Production Supervisor
Erick Tamayo

Production Co-ordinator
Gloria 'Pekas' Lozano
Production Manager
Tita Lombardo
Location Managers
Patricia Cano
Mayte Gallegos
Post-production
Supervisor:
Tlacatéotl Mata
Co-ordinator:
Pablo Baksht Segovia
Production Consultant
Anna Roth Kanarska
Assistant Directors
Carlos Hidalgo
Efrén del Moral
2nd Unit:
Adrián Grümber
Julián 'Chico' Valdés
Script Supervisor
Luciana Kaplan
Casting Director
Manuel Teil
Special Effects
Co-ordinator
Alejandro Vázquez
Graphic Design
Luis Blackaller
Consultant Editors
Guillermo del Toro
Carlos Bolado
Art Director
Melo Hinojosa
Art Department
Co-ordinator
Alisarine Ducolomb
Set Decorator
Julieta Alvarez

Storyboard and
Making-of
Fernando Llanos
Costume Design
Gabriela Diaque
Wardrobe Head
STPC:
Ismael Jardón Texas
Stylist
Gabriel Solana
Make-up
David Gameros
Marco Rosado
Hairdressers
Isabel Amezcua
Eduardo Gómez
Front Credits Design
Oliver Castro
End Credits Design
Pablo Rovalo
Ignacio Borja
Music Supervisor
Lynn Fainchtein
Soundtrack
'La vida es un carnaval',
Celia Cruz; 'Sí señor',
Control Machete;
'Lucha de gigantes',
Nacha Pop;
'Corazón', Titán;
'Dame el poder', Banda
Espuela de Oro;
'Coolo', Illya Kuryaki
and the Valderramas;
'Long Cool Woman in a
Black Dress', the Hollies;
'La cumbia del garrote',
Los del Garrote;
'Lucha de gigantes', Fiebre.

Sound Design
Martín Hernández
Sound Supervisors
Martín Hernández
Roland N. Thai
Sound
Antonio Diego
Final Mix Engineers
Geoffrey G. Rubay
Rudi Pi
Sound Editors
Joaquín Díaz
Efraín García Mora
Alejandro Quevedo
Rodolfo Romero
Adrián Reynoso
Sound Effects Recordists
Martín Hernández
Carlos Honc
Samuel Mendoza
Kaeri Tedla
Stunt Co-ordinators
Gerardo Moreno
Vehicles:
Edgar Lezama 'Chivata'
Dog Trainers
Larry Casanova
Ernesto Aparicio

Cast
Emilio Echevarría
El Chivo
Gael García
Octavio
Goya Toledo
Valeria
Alvaro Guerrero
Daniel
Vanessa Bauche
Susana
Jorge Salinas
Luis
Marco Pérez
Ramiro
Rodrigo Murray
Gustavo
Humberto Busto
Jorge
Gerardo Campbell
Mauricio
Rosa María Bianchi
Aunt Luisa
Dunia Saldívar
Susana's mother
Adriana Barraza
Octavio's mother
José Sefami
Leonardo
Lourdes Echevarría
Maru
Laura Almela
Julieta
Ricardo Dalmacci
Andrés Salgado
Gustavo Sánchez Parra
El Jarocho
Dagoberto Gama
Alvaro

Gustavo Muñoz
El Chispas
Carlo Bernal
Javier
Rodrigo Obstab
El Jaibo
Edgar González
baby Rodrigo
Hilda González
cashier
Patricio Castillo
doctor
Roberto Medina
male TV presenter
Angeles Marín
female TV presenter
Ana María González
nurse
Carlos Samperio
man at scrap yard
T. Kazuyo Togawa
fat lady
Gema Aparicio
domestic
Adriana Varone
Luis's lover
Bruno Salgado
Champignon
Adriana Islas
Lina
Regina Abad
Jimena
Leoncio Torres
El Pelón
Luisa Geliz
Daniel's secretary
Jean Paul Bierry
man in meeting
Alma Rocío González
woman in meeting

Mauricio Martínez
police agent
Juan Manuel Ramos
policeman
Ernesto Bog
José Luis Barraza
men
Jorge Arellano
Jonathan Herrera
children minding car
Heriberto Castillo
stranger

Certificate
18
Distributor
Optimum Releasing

13,817 feet
153 minutes 32 seconds

Dolby
In Colour
Subtitles

Mexican theatrical title
Amores perros

Credits compiled by
Markku Salmi,
BFI Filmographic Unit

Bibliography

I would like to thank Martha Sosa of Altavista for generously providing access to unpublished sources, including the shooting script, press and publicity files, and materials used for art design and location scouting.

The original Spanish script remains unpublished. Readers of the English translation should be aware that it contains some basic errors (e.g. 'persecución' [chase] is rendered as 'persecution') and differs considerably from the final cut of the film. The UK DVD (Optimum, 2001) has numerous extras including a director's commentary on deleted sequences. The double CD (Universal/Surco, 2000) includes music inspired by the film, as well as the soundtrack.

Below are listed only items relating to the film or Mexican audiovisual culture. For other works cited in the text see Notes. Full references to press materials, including author, are given only for major articles or interviews. Minor press reports are cited in the text with source and date of publication. The press sources for the prologue are from the week 8–15 February 2002: La Jornada (left-wing daily); El Heraldo (right-wing daily); El Economista (financial daily); TVyNovelas (gossip weekly); Teleguía (TV listings weekly); Letras Libres (culture monthly).

Altavista, Amores perros/Amours chiennes/Love's a Bitch [Cannes pressbook], 2000.

Arriaga, Guillermo, Un dulce olor a muerte (Madrid: Planeta, 1994).

—— 'Perro negro/perro blanco' [unpublished shooting script, with corrections by hand], 30 March 1999.

—— Amores Perros [script], trans. Alan Page (London: Faber, 2001).

Arroyo, José, review of Amores Perros, Sight and Sound, May 2001, pp. 39–40.

Audé, Françoise, 'Désirs aveugles, fantômes futurs' [review and interview with Alejandro González Iñárritu], Positif no. 477, November 2000, pp. 22–8.

Ayala Blanco, Jorge, La fugacidad del cine mexicano (Mexico City: Océano, 2001).

Berg, Charles Ramírez, Cinema of Solitude: A Critical Study of Mexican Film, 1967–1983 (Austin: University of Texas, 1992).

Centro de Capacitación Cinematográfica, 1975–2000 (Mexico: CONACULTA, 2001).

Chumo II, Peter N., 'Script Review: Amores Perros', Creative Screenwriting vol. 8 no. 2, March–April 2001, pp. 10–12.

Cueva, Álvaro, Sangre de mi sangre: verdades y mentiras de las telenovelas en América Latina (Mexico City: Plaza y Janés, 2001).

de la Fuente, Anna Marie, 'Case Study: Amores Perros', Screen International no. 1315, 6–12 July 2001, p. 17.

—— 'Territory Focus: Mexico', Screen International no. 1345, 22–8 February 2002, pp. 12–13.

García Canclini, Néstor (ed.), Los nuevos espectadores: cine, televisión, y video en México (Mexico City: IMCINE/CONACULTA, 1994).

García Tsao, Leonardo, 'Elogios a Amores Perros' [Cannes location report], La Jornada, 15 May 2000.

—— 'After the Breakthrough of Amores Perros, What's Next for Mexican Cinema?', Film Comment vol. 37 no. 4 (2001), pp. 11–13.

King, John, Magical Reels, second edn. (London: Verso, 2000).

Le Monde, 'L'Amour, chien de l'enfer des villes' [review of Amores Perros], 1 November 2000, p. 29.

Monsiváis, Carlos, 'Mythologies', in Paulo Antonio Paranaguá (ed.), Mexican Cinema (London: BFI, 1995), pp. 117–27.

Oppenheimer, Jean, 'A Dog's Life' [interview with Rodrigo Prieto], American Cinematographer vol. 82 no. 4, April 2001, pp. 20–9.

Optimum Releasing, 'Amores Perros Wins BAFTA' [press release] (London), 26 February 2002.

Pedroza, Carlos and Alfonso Flores-Durán, 'Amores perros: a la pelea con los críticos de Cannes', Cine XS, June 2000, pp. 34–5.

Pérez Soler, Bernardo, 'Pup Fiction' [interview with Alejandro González Iñárritu], Sight and Sound, May 2001, pp. 29–30.

Romney, Jonathan, 'Going to the Dogs' [interview with Alejandro González Iñárritu], Guardian, 22 August 2000, section 2, pp. 12–13.

Stratton, David, review of Amores Perros, Variety, 22–8 May 2000, p. 24.

Torres San Martín, Patricia, 'Los perros amores de los tapatíos' [research paper on audiences in Guadalajara], unpublished.

Also Published

L'Argent
Kent Jones (1999)

Blade Runner
Scott Bukatman (1997)

Blue Velvet
Michael Atkinson (1997)

Caravaggio
Leo Bersani & Ulysse Dutoit
(1999)

A City of Sadness
Bérénice Reynaud (2000)

Crash
Iain Sinclair (1999)

The Crying Game
Jane Giles (1997)

Dead Man
Jonathan Rosenbaum
(2000)

**Dilwale Dulhaniya Le
Jayenge**
Anupama Chopra (2002)

Don't Look Now
Mark Sanderson (1996)

Do the Right Thing
Ed Guerrero (2001)

Easy Rider
Lee Hill (1996)

The Exorcist
Mark Kermode (1997,
2nd edn 1998)

Eyes Wide Shut
Michel Chion (2002)

Heat
Nick James (2002)

Independence Day
Michael Rogin (1998)

Jaws
Antonia Quirke (2002)

Last Tango in Paris
David Thompson (1998)

**Once Upon a Time in
America**
Adrian Martin (1998)

Pulp Fiction
Dana Polan (2000)

The Right Stuff
Tom Charity (1997)

**Saló or The 120 Days of
Sodom**
Gary Indiana (2000)

Seven
Richard Dyer (1999)

The Silence of the Lambs
Yvonne Tasker (2002)

The Terminator
Sean French (1996)

Thelma & Louise
Marita Sturken (2000)

The Thing
Anne Billson (1997)

**The 'Three Colours'
Trilogy**
Geoff Andrew (1998)

Titanic
David M. Lubin (1999)

Trainspotting
Murray Smith (2002)

The Usual Suspects
Ernest Larsen (2002)

The Wings of the Dove
Robin Wood (1999)

**Women on the Verge of a
Nervous Breakdown**
Peter William Evans (1996)

**WR – Mysteries of the
Organism**
Raymond Durgnat (1999)

BFI Modern Classics combine careful research with high-quality writing about contemporary cinema.

If you would like to receive further information about future **BFI Modern Classics** or about other books from BFI Publishing, please fill in your name and address and return this card to us.*

(No stamp required if posted in the UK, Channel Islands, or Isle of Man.)

NAME

ADDRESS

POSTCODE

WHICH **BFI MODERN CLASSIC** DID YOU BUY?

* In USA and Canada, please return your card to:
University of California Press, 2120 Berkeley Way,
Berkeley, CA 94720 USA

BFI Publishing
21 Stephen Street
FREEPOST 7
LONDON
W1E 4AN